BABY NAMES: THE COMPLETE BOOK OF THE BEST BABY NAMES

Thousands of Names – Most Popular Names of 2015/2016 – Name Meanings & Origins – Top 10 Names of All Times

-Discover Different Methods for Finding the Ideal Name for Your Baby-

- SECOND EDITION -

By Ellen Warren

Introduction

Naming your baby is the first step to getting to know them. Figuring out the perfect name can be exciting—but also overwhelming—there are so many options! If you're reading this book because you don't know where to start (or you've already started and don't know what to do next), relax. You aren't alone; <u>many</u> prospective parents feel just the way you do!

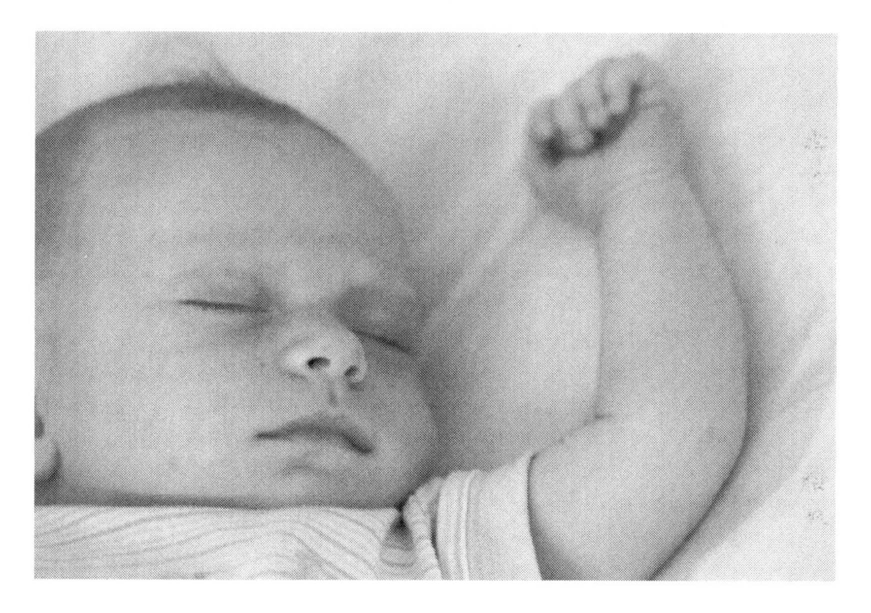

Many factors can come into play when deciding on a name – some of which most parents don't even consider. For example, the name may look great on paper, but is it easy to say out loud? What would your child's spell out if you chose this name? What famous people would they share this name with? Is your child's prospective name too similar to (or the exact same as) a sibling's or cousin's name?

At the end of the day, there is no wrong name for your baby. Some parents like to consider every factor before settling on a name; others take a simpler approach. Whatever name you end up with is perfect. Remember, this is your first gift to your soon-to-be bundle of joy!

Every parent has their own intuitions about naming their baby. You may get “helpful” suggestions from people with different tastes, selection methods, and thought-processes. Smile at them and go about your business of finding your own way. Rely on this book for inspiration and guidance and you will find the path that works for you.

Now, with all that in mind, let’s get started. And remember – have fun!

TABLE OF CONTENTS

Chapter 1: Ten Ways to Name Your Baby

Are you overwhelmed? Do you need a way to narrow things down? With a seemingly infinite list of possible names, choosing just one for your precious baby might feel like an impossible task. Here are some common (and not-so-common) ways people choose baby names.

Meaning

The meanings of names are more than just "conversation starters" for people. The name you choose for your baby can contain a sentiment for them to remember every day of their life. This method is the reverse of "choosing a name and finding out its meaning"; many websites allow you to search for names that match specific meanings. Pick a word that means something to you (or describes the kind of child you'd like to raise) and see what you can discover.

Origin

Do you have a proud heritage? Consider narrowing down your list of baby names by origin. Italian, English, and Celtic names are among the most popular of all names.

Religion

Many of the most popular names come from the Bible. If you're religious (or simply prefer more traditional-sounding names) look to your religion for inspiration.

Remembrance

Naming your child after a relative who has passed away is a great way to remember them. Remember - a name doesn't have to be identical to be a remembrance; consider alternative spellings, variations, and others ways to make your baby's name special <u>and</u> unique.

Homage

Consider naming your child after someone who made a difference in your (or their) life. This could be a friend, a family member, a doctor, or even a celebrity. Perhaps you can choose the name of a musician whose music was the soundtrack of your baby's development.

Just Wait

Stop overthinking. Don't worry. Just wait. See what name comes to you when you see your baby for the first time. Sometimes, the need to make a decision in the spur of the moment draws out ideas you hadn't even considered. As long as both parents are okay with this method, the result can be special—even magical—almost as if your baby chose their own name.

Places

Cheyenne. Dakota. Paris. Troy. These place names are very popular baby names. Remember, you aren't limited to these common place names – consider picking a place with sentimental value for you (such as a place you and your partner visited on your honeymoon). Who knows—you might even start a new baby name trend!

Last Name First

Do you feel like you've exhausted all of the first names on your list? Well, start looking at last names! This is a fairly recent trend; may parents have chosen names like Johnson, Monroe, and Baker, for their children. You can also combine this method with "remembrance"; for example, how would your great grandmother's maiden name sound as a first name? Or would the last name of your favorite singer be just right?

Middle Name

What if you've narrowed your list down to three names – but can't choose between them? If you can't, maybe you shouldn't. You can always use one as a first name and two as a middle name—or even combine two of them with a hyphen to create a special first name.

Systematic Methods

If you can't pick a name *or* a method, there's only one solution left: let fate decide. Systematic methods remove choice from the equation altogether. The most obvious method, of course, is to find a long list of names (such as the ones in this book) and choose one at random with an online random number generator. If you would like *some* degree of choice, make a list of 10 random names and pick your favorite.

You can make systematic methods more sentimental by waiting until a special day to generate your random number, such as your anniversary or your baby's birthdate. Also, instead of a random number, you could use your favorite (or "lucky") number, the average of both parents' favorite numbers, or the date of a special events (i.e., May 9th is 5/09 or 509).

Chapter 2: Is This Really the Right Name for Your Baby?

As important as it is to find that perfect name, remember that even the best names may not be as good as they seem at first. If you think you've found yourself a winner, put it to the test in the following ways. If it clears each of these hurdles, you just might have found the one!

The Nickname Test

This is a classic test, but it's a hard one to gauge. Due to the input of aunts, uncles, and kids in the schoolyard, almost any name can attract an unwanted nickname. However, you can still learn a lot by examining a name's potential for nicknames.

If you select a longer name, be aware that a short form will often be adopted by close friends and family. While you may love your child's full name, you may not find its shortened version nearly as appealing. While this may not matter to you it's still worth considering: Meredith can become Mer, Gwendolyn can become Wendy, and Richard can become Dick.

It may also be a good idea to consider how well this shortened version goes with your last name. It's entirely possible that, on top of not going well with your last name, a short nickname may spell out (or sound out) something embarrassing.

The Initials Test

It is also a good idea to consider the initials of potential names to be. Some names will bring a smile to your face, like Sarah Andrea Donaldson, until you spell out the initials.

A number of people can probably count on one hand the number of times that they've had to use their full initials in their day-to-day life, but this is merely something else to consider.

Monograms (where the last initial is flanked by the first and middle initials) may also be something to consider. As this is one of the more public and readily visible depictions of a person's initials, it may be wise to avoid an arrangement that might attract too much attention.

The Spelling Test

"How do you spell that again?"

"Am I pronouncing this right?"

While unique names and variations can help your child stand out from the crowd, you may want to consider whether or not your child will be haunted by these questions throughout their life. Non-phonetic names, surprise silent letters, and uncommon variations of common names can lead to a lifetime of misspellings and confusion.

A good way to test this is to try it out on other people. See how they pronounce it when you write out the name, or see how they write it down when you say it. If you find people are off the mark more often than they are on, you may want to take this into consideration.

However, like most of the tests described here, it is up to you to decide if this is actually a concern.

The Popularity Test

Some people are thrilled about a particular name until they realize just how popular it is across the continent. If this is something you think you could find yourself worrying about, it doesn't hurt to check with the online Social Security Administration database to see just how popular this name actually is.

There are a number of resources available on their website, including popularity rankings of baby names within specific states.

Some people refuse to choose a name that is in or near the top ten, wanting something more unique for their child. A less common name may save from confusion in classrooms, and may allow their child to stand out.

A sudden rise in popularity may also warn you of pop culture surges. It may be that the unique name that you chose was recently given to the child of a celebrity, and has since spurred a generation of similarly named babies. Some parents may not appreciate this kind of association.

The Pairing Test

This test if for directed towards those who are interested in having multiple children. While it may not immediately spring to mind, you are going to be using your children's names together quite a lot. It only makes sense that they should sound alright together.

Some parents try to keep their children's names somewhat equitable. They try to avoid pairing flowery name choices with simpler options, like Anastasia and Ed for example. Of course, while this may seem like an odd combination to some people, that may be just what you're looking for.

The Email Handle Test

This is a digital world we are living in, and a forward-thinking parent might take into consideration their children's potential email handles. Many professional and school-related emails use a person's first initial and last name.

Depending on this pairing, your child could wind up with an unintentionally embarrassing email address that will follow them through their professional life. This won't be a problem for everyone, but just think of poor Uther Glee.

The Google Test

This may seem like a silly thing to do, but this will give you an idea of both the popularity of your child's name as well as its notoriety.

Unbeknownst to you, the name you have chosen could be shared by some rather big names that are involved in some rather unsavory activities. It may create some associations that you aren't entirely comfortable with.

The Meaning Test

If you are really stuck between options, one test that you might consider doing is researching the meanings behind these names. It may be that you only find one of the meanings to meet your own special criteria, whether that's a name that represents strength, loyalty, or something much more unique.

Name etymologies are quite accessible these days, with countless available through online databases. There are even a few popular etymologies here in this book, for your convenience.

Don't Panic

Remember – these are merely a few points to consider when choosing your baby's name. If anything, they will hopefully help you to narrow down a few of your choices and make your life, as complicated as it may seem right now, a little simpler.

Also, if you are truly in love with a name, don't let these tests get in the way of way of what you truly want. In the end, the best person to judge a potential name's quality is you.

What <u>Not</u> to Worry About

Now that we've covered a few of the things that you may want to consider, here are a few things that you should really try to not worry about.

Something you may not want to do is to allow yourself to be too swayed or discouraged by other people's opinions. Friends and family can be a contrary bunch, even if they don't mean to be. For every positive comment, there can be two not-so-positive comments on the tips of their tongues.

They will have their reasons for liking or disliking names. Some parents and grandparents may be of a more traditional background and pressure you to choose a name that either abides by your heritage or by the trends of the time.

It may very well be that the cultures your friends and family interact with, the media and television they consume are completely different from the cultures that you are at home in.

Some people will question your ideas simply because, "That isn't what I would name my baby."

This doesn't necessarily mean their ideas and comments are useless or invalid. It just means they may not be right for you.

The fact of the matter is, this is your child. You are welcome to heed anyone's opinion, but at the end of the day, the choice is yours and yours alone. Make sure that you and your spouse are comfortable with this name; don't select one that you feel other people have chosen for you.

Also, remember that friends and family often change their opinion of a name once the baby is born.

Sometimes, all people may need is a little time. If you are really set on an obscure name that your parents seem lukewarm about, it may just be that they need time for it to ripen in their minds.

No one will have the passion for a name in the same way that you do. Something that seems insightful and full of meaning to you will fall on deaf ears when you tell it to others. But once they meet your child, you can be sure that they will soon have a reason to consider it special.

In much the same way, you shouldn't you allow yourself to worry about unpleasant name associations.

Even if your spouse is really adamant about a name that turns out to be the name of that miserable manager you worked under one time, or just so happens to be the other half of an unpleasant break-up years ago, your child is its own person. The experiences you have with him or her will override any unpleasantness that you worry might creep in from your past.

If the name is otherwise perfect, you shouldn't let it stop you.

Lastly, you should do all that you can to avoid stressing out. This can be easier said than done. There will be a lot going on, and a lot to prepare for. For some, having to choose a name, on top of everything else that is being demanded of you, can feel like the straw that broke the camel's back.

As stressful as it may seem at first, the fact is, when you finally meet your baby, you'll know you made the right choice. It will seem so natural that it will be hard to imagine having considered any other name.

Chapter 3: The Classics

The Top 10 Boys' Names of All Time

Rank	Name	Origin	Meaning	Famous people
1	James	Hebrew	"Supplanter"	James Baldwin, James Earl Jones, James Brown
2	John	Hebrew	"God is Gracious"	John Oliver, John Coltrane, John Lennon
3	Robert	German	"Bright Fame"	Robert Frost, Robert Kennedy, Robert Pattinson
4	Michael	Hebrew	"Who is Like God"	Michael Jackson, Michael Phelps, Michael Jordan
5	William	English (derived from German)	"Resolute Protection"	William Shakespeare, Prince William
6	David	Hebrew	"Beloved"	David Hasselhoff, David Beckham, David Copperfield
7	Richard	German	"Dominant Ruler"	Richard Pryor, Richard Avedon, Richard Wagner

8	Joseph	Hebrew	“He Will Add”	Joseph Gordon-Levitt, Joseph Haydn
9	Charles	French	“Free Man”	Charles Darwin, Charles Dickens, Prince Charles
10	Thomas	Aramaic	“Twin”	Thomas Jefferson, Tom Hanks, Thomas Paine

The Top 10 Girls' Names of All Time

Rank	Name	Origin	Meaning	Famous people
1	Mary	Hebrew	"Wished-For Child"	Virgin Mary, Mary J. Blige, Mary Tyler Moore
2	Patricia	Latin	"Noble"	Patricia Arquette, Patricia Neal, Patricia Richardson
3	Jennifer	Welsh	"White Shadow" or "White Wave"	Jennifer Lawrence, Jennifer Aniston, Jennifer Lopez
4	Elizabeth	Hebrew	"Pledged to God"	Elizabeth Taylor, Elizabeth Olsen, Queen Elizabeth
5	Linda	German, Spanish	"Serpent" or "Pretty"	Linda Ronstadt, Linda Gray
6	Barbara	Latin	"Traveler From a Foreign Land"	Barbra Streisand, Barbara Eden
7	Susan (Short for Susannah)	Hebrew	"Lily"	Susan B. Anthony, Susan Sarandon, Susan

				Lucci
8	Margaret	Greek	“Pearl”	Margaret Thatcher, Margaret Cho, Margaret Rimes (LeAnn Rimes)
9	Jessica	Hebrew	“Wealthy”	Jessica Biel, Jessica Alba, Jessica Simpson, Jessica Capshaw
10	Sarah	Hebrew	“Princess”	Sarah Michelle Gellar, Sarah Silverman

Chapter 4: Modern Favorites

Today's Most Popular Boys' Names

1. Noah

The name Noah can mean “rest” or “comfort”. When used in in reference to the biblical Noah, (the builder of the Ark), it means “wanderer.” This English name is one of many soft-sounding names to become popular in recent years. “Noah” started to become popular in 2009; in 2013, it nudged “Jacob” out of first place.

As an Old Testament name, Noah may sound very traditional. However, the famous ark-builder is only one of many famous Noahs. Noah Webster is famous for his linguistics and education work—and of course the Merriam-Webster dictionary. The actor, Noah Munck, is well-known among many young people.

2. Liam

Liam means "resolute protection". This Irish name is a derivative of William, and is often used as a short version or nickname for boys with that name. Like several of today's top boys' names, Liam only became popular a few years ago. Now, it's even more popular than its original form, William.

The name Liam gained most of its popularity from celebrities. Liam Neeson, the Irish actor, is the most famous. Liam Payne – a member of the band One Direction – helped the name stay appealing to younger generations.

3. Mason

Mason is an English name that began as an occupation title and last name. A mason is someone who works with stone, and in Old English the word "macian" means "to make." It's a name that predicts an industrious childhood full of building blocks and Lego houses.

The name Mason is full of celebrity representation – especially among celebrities' children. Cuba Gooding Jr. and Melissa Joan Hart both have children named Mason. There is a comedian and composer named Mason Williams, as well as a couple of fictional characters with the name from recent television series.

4. Jacob

Few names can hold a candle to Jacob when it comes to popularity in modern times. It slowly rose to popularity in the 90s, then in 1999 it became the most popular name for an incredible 13 year streak. It is a biblical Hebrew name – the name of the grandfather of the twelve tribes of Israel – but its religious connotations have largely faded away. The meaning is "supplanter" – someone who takes something by their own means.

Late in its popularity streak, Jacob got a boost in interest and also rekindled interest in the younger generation thanks to the Twilight book and movie series character. A more classical famous Jacob is Jacob Grimm, one half of the Brothers Grimm behind Grimm's Fairy Tales.

5. William

Classic and modern all at once, William is a timeless name that means "resolute protection." Among the most famous people named William are: legendary playwright William Shakespeare; William Gates (better known as Bill Gates); Prince William; and various leaders, including dozens of kings and a few U.S. Presidents. It is an English name heavily rooted in nobility, although it has German origins (from Wilhelm).

Variants or nicknames of William include: Will, Willem, Bill, Billy, and Liam. Wilma and Willa are popular female versions.

6. Ethan

Yet another biblical Hebrew name, Ethan is most popular in the United Kingdom and United States partially thanks to the *Mission Impossible* movies' protagonist, Ethan Hunt. Ethan is one of the most repeated names in the Old Testament of the Bible, giving it plenty of associations with virtues, particularly wisdom. The name itself means "strong" or "firm."

Other famous Ethans include: Ethan Frome (protagonist of the self-titled novel by Edith Wharton), Revolutionary War hero Ethan Allen, and actor Ethan Hawke.

7. Michael

Michael is another timeless name like William that seems to be popular all the time. In fact, it held the number one spot for about 50 years. It is a Hebrew name – and a very important one in the Bible, as it is the name of Archangel Michael. Other famous Michaels in more modern times include Michael Phelps, Michael Jordon, Michael Jackson, and Mike Shinoda.

Nicknames and variations of Michael include: Mike, Mikey, Mickey, and Mitchell. Also consider the international variations Mikhail and Miguel.

8. Alexander

Alexander is easily one of the most prevalent names in history in its many forms. From Alexander came Alex, Alec, Zander (or Xander), Zan, and female variations such as Alexandria, Alexis, Lexie, and so-on. The name Alexander is Greek, and means "protector of the people."

Many great figures in history bear this name: Alexander Graham Bell, the inventor of the first practical telephone; Alexander the Great; and the English poet, Alexander Pope.

9. James

As the number one most popular name of all time in the United States, it's no surprise that James is still holding strong in 2015. It is, after all, the name of kings, presidents, apostles in the Bible, writers, actors, and musicians – the list goes on. Interestingly, few of the variations or nicknames of James are nearly as popular, so parents seeking something unique could turn to those. It is an English name that began as a derivation of Jacob.

Nicknames of James include: Jamie, Jamesy, Jim, Jimmy, Jameson, Jem; international versions include Diego, Jaap, Jacques, Shamus, Giacomo, and Santiago.

10. Daniel

Last but not least, Daniel finishes off the top 10 names of 2015 as yet another biblical Hebrew name. It means "God is my judge," or essentially someone who believes in the morals of the Christian faith. This name seems to fluctuate in popularity often. Some famous Daniels:

Daniel Radcliffle (Harry Potter), Daniel Handler (Lemony Snicket), Daniel Boone, and plenty of fictional examples in popular culture.

Nicknames and versions in other languages include Danny, Dan, Dane, Dano, Nelo, and their feminine counterpart, Danielle.

Today's Most Popular Girls' Names

1. Emma

The name Emma is a German name meaning "all-embracing" or "universal" – someone who is very accepting and understanding. The popularity of this name in recent years is no doubt thanks to celebrities Emma Stone, Emma Roberts, and Emma Watson, as well as its frequent use for the name of fictional protagonists.

Despite its current popularity, Emma is actually a very old name which first gained notice from royalty over a thousand years ago. It was at the top of the list in the 1800s, but fell steadily in the 1900s until the 80s.

There are plenty of derived or alternate versions of this name, such as Emily, Emilia, Amelie, and Ella.

2. Olivia

Olivia is associated with the olive tree, which is a symbol of peace and fertility. It is a French name with Latin roots, first popularized by William Shakespeare's play *Twelfth Night*. In the United States, this name only recently made its splash. Many of the better known Olivias are either characters in television or actresses: Olivia Benson (Law & Order SVU), Olivia Munn, and Olivia Wilde, to name a few.

Alternate names for Olivia include Olive, Liv, and Livia.

3. Sophia

This Greek name meaning "wisdom" is recently popular name which is seemingly just as common in fiction as it is in reality. The first major figure named Sophia had an interesting idea for names herself: St. Sophia ("wisdom") had three daughters named Love, Hope, and Faith. Alternate versions or nicknames include Sophie/Sofie, Sofia, Zofia, Saffi, Fifi, or the Italian version Sofonisba.

4. Isabella

Isabella is a Spanish and Italian name meaning "pledged to God." It was derived from the Hebrew name Elizabeth, although it has since found its way into a wide variety of cultures. Though the Twilight series character Isabella Swan undoubtedly boosted this name's popularity considerably, it has deep roots throughout history. Shakespeare's *Measure for Measure* features an Isabella, and various queens had this name.

Isabella is also diverse when it comes to nicknames: Izzy, Isa, and Bella. Isobel, Isabel, and Isabelle are a few interesting variations.

5. Ava

Ava is a simple Latin name derived from the biblical Eve. It means "life" and has roots just as old as Emma. The surge in popularity for Ava came from a number of celebrities choosing the name for their daughters, such as Hugh Jackman and Reese Witherspoon.

Ava has plenty of variations to choose from if you like the name but want to make it unique: Ada, Eva, Aveline, and Avery. The name Aveline can be compared to Evelyn, possibly making Ava a nickname as well.

6. Mia

With the first wave of Mias coming in the 60s thanks to actress Mia Farrow, this is certainly a modern name. It is an Italian name meaning "mine" or "bitter," and can be considered a short form of Maria. Thanks to its simplicity, it's a great choice for those who want a feminine name that is both elegant and humble.

Other famous Mias include Kate Winslet's daughter and actress Mia Sara.

7. Emily

Although related to the #1 name Emma, Emily is not in fact its proper form. Emily is its own name, a female version of the Latin Emil meaning "eager." It's a classic name, easy to say, popular among celebrities, and seemingly everywhere in popular culture. Some examples include the poet Emily Dickinson, Emily (now Emma) Watson, author Emily Bronte, and Emily the Strange.

Emily is extremely easy to adapt, shorten, and derive – it's easily one of the most versatile names around. Some alternate versions and nicknames (many of which overlap with Emma's) are: Amelie, Amelia, Mila, Emi, and Emiliana.

8. Abigail

Abigail is a Hebrew name from the Old Testament which means

"father's joy." In the Bible, Abigail was a beautiful and wise prophet. The name became a nickname for maids in the 1800s, but thanks to some famous faces, it made a comeback. The nickname Abby is arguably seen more often on TV and in movies than its proper form, such as in the TV show NCIS or the movie The Lovely Bones.

Some famous real-life instances of the name Abigail are: actress Abigail Breslin, First Lady Abigail Adams, and Abigail Williams.

9. Madison

Madison, an English name meaning "good," was actually originally a boy's name which also simply meant "son of Maud." Until the 80s, it was a pretty low-density name, but when the movie *Splash* featured a mermaid named Madison it started to climb. From 1997 to 2014 it bounced around in the top 10. Addison is a similar name which has become a popular alternative despite not actually having the same roots.

Variants and nicknames for Madison include ending the name in –syn or –sen instead of –son; Mattison; and Madsen. Actress Madison Riley is one of the most famous contemporary examples of this name.

10. Charlotte

Rounding out the top 10 female baby names of 2015 is the French name Charlotte, which means petite or womanly. This name has popular culture to thank for its rise in numbers, as many celebrities named their children Charlotte in recent years, such as Sarah Michelle Gellar and Colin Hanks. Characters named Charlotte have also appeared in major films, such as the one played by Scarlett Johansson in *Lost in Translation*. Two famous Charlottes in real life are Charlotte Bronte and Princess Charlotte of Cambridge.

Nicknames of Charlotte include Charlie, Lottie, Tottie, and Lola.

Chapter 5: Celebrity Names

Some people look to celebrities to for inspiration, and for good reason. Whether it's their own artistic spirit or a desire to test the boundaries of social norms, the children of celebrities can often find themselves with some rather interesting and unusual names. Here's a small list of some of the more off-beat names that celebrities have chosen to endow their offspring with.

Famous Boys' Names

Name of Child	**Parents**	**Meaning of First Name**
Apollo Bowie Flynn Rossdale	Gwen Stefani and Gavin Rossdale	"Strength" (Indo-European); "God of Sun and Light" (Greek)
Arlo Day Brody	Leighton Meester and Adam Brody	"Between Two Highlands" (Gaelic)
Arlo Robert Galafassi	Toni Collette and David Galafassi	"Between Two Highlands" (Gaelic)
Atlas Norton	Ed Norton and Shauna Robertson	"Not enduring" (Greek); "Titan Who Supports the Heavens" (Greek)
Audio Science Clayton	Shannyn Sossamon	"Of or Relating to

	and Dallas Clayton	Audible Sound" (Rooted in Latin)
Aurelius Cy Andrea Busson	Elle Macpherson and Arpad Busson	"Golden" or "Gilded" (Latin); A Roman Emperor and philosopher
Axl Jack Duhamel	Josh Duhamel and Fergie	Medieval Danish form of Absalom; "My Father is Peace"
Bear Winslet	Kate Winslet and Ned Rocknroll	From the name of the animal
Bingham Hawn Bellamy	Kate Hudson and Matt Bellamy	"Homestead at a Hollow" (British)
Bodhi Ransom Green	Megan Fox and Briar Austin Green	"Awakened" or "Knowing" Consciousness (Indian)
Booker Jombe Parker	Thandie Newton and Ol Parker	"Maker of Books"; Famous African-American leader
Bronx Mowgli Wentz	Ashlee Simpson and Pete Wentz	A Borough of New York; "Broken Land" (Dutch)
Brooklyn Beckham	Victoria and	A Borough of New York;

	Victoria Beckham	"Broken Land" (Dutch)
Buddy Bear Maurice Oliver	Jamie Oliver and Jools Oliver	"Friend" (English)
Cyrus Michael Christopher Dancy	Claire Danes and Hugh Dancy	"Far-Sighted" or "Young" (Greek/Persian)
Denim Braxton-Lewis	Toni Braxton and Keri Lewis	From the name of the fabric
Diezel Braxton-Lewis	Toni Braxton and Keri Lewis	Alternate spelling of "Diesel"
Egypt Daoud Ibarr Dean	Alicia Keys and Kaseem Dean	From the name of the country
Ever Imre Morissette-Treadway	Alanis Morissette and Mario Treadway	Possible contraction of "Ever in Life" (Old English)
Gene Gallagher	Liam Gallagher and Nicole Appleton	Contraction of Eugene; "Well-Born" (Greek)
Gulliver Flynn Oldman	Gary Oldman and Lesley Manville	Possibly "Glutton" (English/French)

Gunner Flowers	Brandon Flowers and Tana Flowers	Cannoneer; derived from "Cautious in War" (Old Norse)
Homer James Jigme Gere	Richard Gere and Carey Lowell	"Hostage" or "Pledge" (Greek); A Greek poet
Hopper Jack Penn	Sean Penn and Robin Wright	Adapted from a surname meaning "Acrobatic"
Ignatius Martin Upton	Cate Blanchett and Martin Upton	"Fire" (Latin)
Ikhyd Edgar Arular Bronfman	M.I.A. (rapper) and Benjamin Brewer	"Strong Connection" (Arabic)
Indio Falconer Downey	Robert Downey Jr and Deborah Falconer	Variant of "Indigo", a purplish dye; "India"
Jermajesty Jackson	Jermaine Jackson and Alejandra Oaziza	Possibly contraction of Jermaine and "Majesty"
Kahekili Kali	Evangeline Lilly and Norman Kali	"Thunder" (Hawaiian)
Kai Wayne Rooney	Wayne Rooney and	"Sea" (Hawaiian); "Victory" (Mandarin);

	Coleen Rooney	"Unbreakable" (Burmese)
Kal-El Cage	Nicholas Cage and Alice Kim	Superman's given name
Keen Ruffalo	Mark Ruffalo and Sunrise Coigney	"Bold" or "Brave" (Old English)
Kyd Miller Duchovny	David Duchovny and Téa Leoni	Alternate spelling of "Kid"
Lennon Gallagher	Liam Gallagher and Patsy Kensit	"Lover" (Irish)
Livingston Alves McConaughey	Matthew McConaughey and Camila Alves	"Leving's town"(Middle English)
Marquise Jackson	50 Cent and Shanique Tompkins	Title of rank (European)
Memphis Eve Hewson	Bono and Alison Hewson	"Abode of the Good" (Hebrew)
Milan Piqué Mebarak	Shakira and Gerard Piqué	"Gracious" or "Dear" (Slavic); "Middle of the Plain" (Latin)

Morocco Elijah Tyson	Mike Tyson and Lakina Spicer Tyson	From the country
Ocean Whitaker	Forest Whitaker	From the geographic feature
Otis Alexander Sudeikis	Olivia Wilde and Jason Sudeikis	"Wealth" or "Fortune" (German)
Phinnaeus Walter Moder	Julia Roberts and Daniel Moder	Alternate spelling of Phinehas; "Serpent's Mouth" (Hebrew)
Phyllon Joy Gorré	Doutzen Kroes (model) and Sunnery James	"Foliage" or "Leaf" (Ancient Greek)
Pilot Inspektor Riesgraf Lee	Jason Lee and Beth Riesgraf	From a track by the indie band Grandaddy
Rex Rayne Wood	Fearne Cotton and Jesse Wood	"King" (Latin)
Sailor Gene Gardner	Liv Tyler and Dave Garder	From the occupation
Saint Lazslo	Pete Wentz and Meagan Camper	"Holy" (Latin); from the religious figures

Satchel Lewis Lee	Spike Lee and Tonya Lewis	"Sack" or "Bag" (Old English); from the occupation
Seven Sirius Benjamin	Erykah Badu and Andre 3000	From the number
Silas Randall Timberlake	Jessica Biel and Justin Timberlake	Possible short form of Silvanus; "Wood" or "Forest" (Latin)
Skyler Morrison Berman	Rachel Zoe and Rodger Berman	"Scholar" (Dutch)
Sparrow James Midnight Madden	Nicole Richie and Joel Madden	From the bird; derived from "Spearwa" (Old English)
Tate Jones	Emma Bunton and Jade Jones	Possibly short form of Tatum; "Tata's Homestead" (Old English)
Tennessee James Toth	Reese Witherspoon and Jim Toth	From the name of a Cherokee village
Titan Jewell Witherspoon	Kelly Rowland and Tim Witherspoon	Giants who preceded the Olympian gods (Greek)

Wilder Brooks Hudson	Oliver Hudson and Erinn Bartlett	Exterpolation of "Wild"; "Lose One's Way"; "Perplex"
Zuma Nesta Rock Rossdale	Gwen Stefani and Gavin Rossdale	"Peace" (Arabic)

Famous Girls' Names

Name of Child	Parents	Meaning of First Name
Agnes Lark Bettany	Paul Bettany and Jennifer Connelly	"Chaste" (Latin/Greek)
Alai-Mai Humes	Rochelle Wiseman and Marvin Humes	"Joyful Ocean" (Chinese)
Amba Isis Jackson	Jade Jagger and Piers Jackson	"Mother" (Sanskrit); An Epithet of Parvati (Indian Mythology)
Anaiya Coyle	Nadine Coyle	"Look Up to God" (African)
Apple Blythe Alison Martin	Gwyneth Paltrow and Chris Martin	From the Fruit
Aviana Olea Le Gallo	Amy Adams and Darren Le Gallo	Short form of "Avian"; "Bird-like"
Bear Blu	Alicia Silverstone and Christopher Jarecki	From the name of the animal
Betty Kitten	Jonathan Ross and	Short form of Elizabeth;

	Jane Goldman	"My God is Abundance"; a tribute to Bettie Paige
Birdie Lee Silverstein	Busy Philipps and Marc Silverstein	Possibly short form of Bertha or Bridget; "bright"; "exalted one"
Blue Ivy	Beyoncé and Jay-Z	From the color
Bluebell Madonna Halliwell	Geri Halliwell and Sacha Gervasi	From the flower
Briar Rose Christensen	Rachel Bilson and Hayden Christensen	Pseudonym for Sleeping Beauty
Cleo Buckman Schwimmer	David Schwimmer and Zoe Buckman	Short form of Cleopatra; "Glory of the Father" (Greek)
Coco Riley Arquette	Courtney Cox and David Arquette	A common shortform for names beginning with Co-
Cosima Violet Vaughn Drummond	Claudia Schiffer and Matthew Vaughn	Italian derivation of "Order" or "Decency" (Greek)
Cricket Pearl Silverstein	Busy Philipps and	From the insect; From the sport

	Marc Silverstein	
Daisy True Ryan	Meg Ryan	From the flower
Delilah Genoveva Stewart del Toro	Kimberly Stewart and Benicio del Toro	"Delicate" or "Fragile" (Hebrew); Biblical betrayer of Samson
Destry Allyn Spielberg	Steven Spielberg and Kate Capshaw	Derivation of Destrier; "Warhorse" (French)
Elsie Otter Pechenik	Zooey Deschanel and Jacob Pechenik	Short form of Elizabeth; "My God is Abundance"
Elula Lottie Mirian Cohen	Isla Fisher and Sacha Baron Cohen	Derived from the twelfth month of the Jewish civil year
Emerson Rose Tenney	Teri Hatcher and Jon Tenney	"Son of Emery"; Derived from "Whole" or "Power" (German)
Ever Gabo Anderson	Milla Jovovich and Paul Anderson	Possible contraction of "Ever in Life" (Old English)
Faith Margaret	Keith Urban and	"Trust" (Latin)

Kidman Urban	Nicole Kidman	
Fifi Trixibelle Geldof	Paula Yates and Bob Geldof	Short form of Josephine; Derived from “He Will Add” (Hebrew)
Fox India Owen	Mark Owen and Emma Ferguson	From the animal
Frances Bean Cobain	Courtney Love and Kurt Cobain	“Frenchman” (Latin)
Frankie Barrymore Kopelman	Drew Barrymore and Will Kopelman	Feminine variation of Frank
Fuchsia Katherine Sumner	Sting and Frances Tomelty	From the flower
Gaia Romilly Wise	Emma Thompson and Greg Wise	“Earth” (Greek); Mother goddess of Greek mythology
Happy Hinds	Macy Grey and Tracy Hinds	From the emotion
Harlow Winter Kate Madden	Nicole Richie and Joel Madden	“Rock” or “Army Hill” (Old English)

Harper Seven	David Beckham and Victoria Beckham	Someone who makes or plays harps (Old English)
Harper Willow Grohl	Dave Grohl and Jordyn Blum	Someone who makes or plays harps (Old English)
Haven Garner Warren	Jessica Alba and Cash Warren	"Safe Place" (Old English)
Heavenly Hiraani Tiger Lily Hutchence	Paula Yates and Michael Hutchence	From the spiritual location
Hero Harper Quinn	Myleene Klass and Graham Quinn	"Hero" (Greek); The famed lover of Leander
India Pearl Weinstein	Georgina Chapman (Marchesa designer) and Harvey Weinstein (film mogul)	From the Country; "Body of Trembling Water" or "River" (Sanskrit)
James Reynolds	Blake Lively and Ryan Reynolds	Derived from Jacob; "Supplanter" (Hebrew)
Java Kumala Holloway	Josh Holloway and Yessica Kumala	From the island or the drink
Keeva Jane Denisof	Alyson Hannigan and Alexis Denisof	Derived from Caoimhe; "Beautiful" or "Gentle" (Gaelic)

Locklyn Kyla Vaughn	Vince Vaughn and Kyla Webber	Derived from Lachlan; Nickname for a Norwegian person (Scottish)
Luna Coco Patricia Lampard	Frank Lampard and Elen Rivas	"Moon" (Latin); Roman goddess of the moon
Lyra Cullum	Sophie Dahl and Jamie Cullum	From a constellation in the northern sky
Makena Lei Gordon Carnahan	Helen Hunt and Matthew Carnahan	"Happy One" (Kikuyu)
Marlowe Sturridge	Sienna Miller and om Sturridge	"Remnants of a Lake" (Old English)
Marnie Rose Cooper	Lily Allen and Sam Cooper	"Rejoice" (Hebrew)
Moroccan Scott Cannon	Mariah Carey and Nick Cannon	"Land of God" (Amazigh)
Nahla Ariela Aubry	Halle Berry and Gabriel Aubry	"A Drink of Water" (Arabic)
North West	Kim Kardashian and Kanye West	From the compass points

Princess Tiaamil Andre	Katie Price and Peter Andre	From the royal rank
Reiley Dilys Stella Willis	Stella McCartney and Alasdhair Willis	Alternate spelling of Riley; possibly "Rye Clearing" (Old English)
River Rose	Kelly Clarkson and Brandon Blackstock	"Riverbank" (Old French)
Rosalind Arusha Arkadina Altalune Florence Thurman-Busson	Uma Thurman and Arpad Busson	"Beautiful Rose" (Latin)
Royal Reign	Lil Kim	"King" (Latin)
Sailor Lee Brinkley Cook	Christie Brinkley and Peter Cook	From the occupation
Seraphina Rose Elizabeth Affleck	Ben Affleck and Jennifer Garner	"Fiery One" (Hebrew); An order of angels
Shiloh Nouvel Jolie-Pitt	Brad Pitt and Angelina Jolie	"Tranquil" (Hebrew)

Sunday Rose Urban	Nidole Kidman and Keith Urban	"Sun Day" (Old English)
Sunny Madeline Sandler	Adam Sandler and acqueline Samantha Titone	"Cheerful" (English)
Suri Cruise	Tom Cruise and Katie Holmes	Yiddish variation of Sarah; noblewoman (Hebrew)
Tallulah Belle Willis	Bruce Willis and Demi Moore	"Leaping Waters" (Choctaw); "Rown" (Creek)
Tallulah Pine Le Bon	Simon Le Bon and Yasmin Le Bon	"Leaping Waters" (Choctaw); "Rown" (Creek)
Theodora Rose Williams	Robbie Williams and Ayda Field	Variation on Theodore; "Gift of God" (Greek)
Vida Alves McConaughey	Matthew McConaughey and Camila Alves	"Life" (Latin)
Willow Camille Reign Smith	Will Smith and Jada Pinkett Smith	From the tree (Old English)

Wyatt Isabelle Kutcher	Ashton Kutcher and Mila Kunis	Variation on Old English “Brave Battle”
Wylda Rae Johnson	Aaron Johnson and Sam Taylor Wood	From “Wild” (German)

Chapter 6: Movies, Books, and Television

When books or movies leave their mark on the world, you can always expect a few of the more memorable characters to make it into the lists of popular baby names.

This can be one of those choices, especially when it comes to a particularly unique pop culture reference. There will be a point where you have to ask yourself if, in twenty years, your children will still appreciate your passion for HBO's *Game of Thrones.*

While boy names seem to range all across the board, people have a strong preference for girls' names that refer to strong, capable, and independent female protagonists.

Here is a list of some of the more unique popular references parents have chosen.

Boys' Names from Pop Culture

1. Archer

Archer is the less-than-perfect James Bond of the 21st century. The anti-hero of an American adult animation created by Adam Reed for the FX Network, Archer lives a dysfunctional life while working for an independent spy agency owned by his mother. He injects chaos into the world around him, but he always seems to come out on top.

The name Archer is an English term for "bowman," but it has Old French origins.

2. Emmet

Emmet is the name of the lovable protagonist of *The Lego Movie*, released in 2014. Silly but loyal, he saves his world by sharing with everyone his own special sense of individuality.

Emmet is an English surname that was derived from a diminutive of the name Emma. In turn, Emma found its origins as a short form for similar Germanic names. It meant "whole" or "universal". It was brought to England by the Normans.

3. Gus

Gus has seen a marked rise in popularity since the 2014 release of *The Fault in Our Stars*. A selfless young man who has lost a leg to cancer, Gus, as portrayed by Ansel Elgort, is charming and intelligent, and does the most with what little time he has to share.

Gus is typically a short form for the name Augustus, a Roman name. Augustus means "great" or "venerable". It is derived from a Latin word that means "to increase".

4. Jesse

One of the troubled protagonists from AMC's *Breaking Bad*, there has been a noted rise in Jesse's since the series opening and continued popularity, even now that the series has ended.

Jesse is a Hebrew name which possibly means "gift". This name also has origins in the bible, as Jesse is the father of King David in the Old Testament.

5. Kristoff

Disney's *Frozen* did not steal the hearts of children alone. Many parents have looked to this 2013 animated feature for inspiration. Kristoff, the lower-class love interest for the younger princess, has received some attention. A loner to begin with, he soon shows that he has the makings of a very loyal friend.

Kristoff is a Scandinavian variant of the name Christopher. This is turn finds its roots in the Late Greek name Christophoros, which means "bearing Christ."

6. Logan

The definitive tough guy of the comic book world, Logan (aka Wolverine) has always been a fan favorite in the X-Men universe. A bundle of raw strength and machismo, it's easy to see why. The name itself has become increasingly popular since Hugh Jackman's first portrayal of the character in 2000, reaching a record height of popularity after the 2013 release, *The Wolverine*.

The name Logan has Scottish origins. It was derived from a surname that was in turn derived from a place name that meant "little hollow" in Scottish Gaelic.

7. Loki

While this name originally hails from Norse mythology, the cause for Loki's recent popularity has more to do with comic book movies as well. Played by Tom Hiddleston, Loki has been reintroduced to the modern world as a powerful trickster villain in the 2011 release of *Thor.* This is a role which he very much fulfilled in his mythological roots as well. While it is odd to name a child after a villain, there have been many people willing to take this step.

8. Tyrion

Tyrion Lannister was popularized by the 2011 HBO series *Game of Thrones*. The black sheep of a son in one of the main ruling families, he more than compensates for his short stature with his cunning and intelligence. As one of the rare likable and sort-of good guys, Tyrion, as portrayed by Peter Dinklage, has inspired some people to take up his name.

As the series is rooted in a land known as Westeros, invented by George R. R. Martin, there's no way to trace this name's origins.

9. Olaf

The innocent snowman who just wants to enjoy a summer day, Olaf is another character that has attracted some attention since the release of Disney's *Frozen*. Voiced by Josh Gad, Olaf was as pure as the fresh snow he was made from.

Olaf is a Norwegian name that comes from an Old Norse name that means "ancestor's descendant."

10. Atticus

Many will remember Gregory Peck's portrayal of this iconic childhood hero from *To Kill a Mockingbird*. Atticus is a just and honest man, who manages to succeed at being both a single father and a pillar of society. While Harper Lee's more recent book, *Go Set a Watchman*, debunks this idea of him somewhat, it hasn't stolen the popularity that his name continues to experience.

Atticus stems from a Roman name that means "From Attica" in Latin. Attica is a region in Greece situated around Athens.

Girls' Names from Pop Culture

1. Arya

In *Game of* Thrones, Arya is the rough-and-tumble tomboy of a littlest sister in the ill-fated Stark family. Despite being one of the youngest members of the family, she proves herself more capable than her elders. She survives on her own and lives on her wits for much longer than most people (even those with an army to protect them) can do in this series. She refuses to let herself be stifled by her family; this resilience helps keep her going in the unforgiving world of Westeros.

While this name was likely invented, it may be derived from the Italian word for "song" or "melody".

2. Elsa

The more uniquely named of the two sister-princesses from Disney's *Frozen*, Elsa the Ice Queen is beloved by a generation. Fleeing from home and from her family, she ventured into the snowy peaks around her kingdom to embrace the gift she was taught to despise. A main theme of this movie is accepting yourself and being happy with the person you are.

Elsa is a diminutive form of Elizabeth, which is derived a Hebrew name meaning "My God is an Oath" or "My God is Abundance".

3. Hazel

Hazel is the second half of the love interest in John Greens' *The Fault in Our Stars*. Suffering from cancer and having trouble coming to terms with its progression, she goes to a support group where she has the chance to meet a remarkable fellow. Together, they encourage one another to take chances that both of them would have likely let slip by. Both the movie and the book are emotional works, and the audience is hard pressed to avoid getting attached to her.

The name Hazel adapted from the name for the tree or the light brown color. It is ultimately derived from Old English.

4. Katniss

Katniss Everdeen rekindled the love of dystopian, in Suzanne Collins' *The Hunger Games*, and paved the way for a long line of strong and physically tough female protagonists in ths genre. Stacked against unbeatable odds in a contest with only one winner, she finds some of those things that were missing in her life.

While Katniss has no precise realworld meaning, within *The Hunger Games* it refers to an edible plant that plays a symbolic role in Katniss' life.

5. Khaleesi

Starting off as little more than a bargaining chip for her delusional brother, Khaleesi Daenerys Targaryen comes into her own when becomes a queen of dragons. This is yet another name that people have come to borrow from *Game of Thrones*. Another example of a strong, independent woman, the Khaleesi is always on guard to maintain control over her own destiny, to make up for the years she spent in servitude to her brother and to others.

While Khaleesi has the benefit of meaning "queen" in one of George R. R. Martin's invented languages, this may be an example of one of those pop culture names with a limited shelf life. Cumbersome to pronounce, Khaleesi does not enjoy access to many diminutives that would help distract from such a pointed reference to the series.

6. Maisie

This is the final *Game of Thromes* related name to bring up. It has been so popular that not only are the characters having their names borrowed, the actresses are too. Maisie Williams is best known for her role as Arya Stark. She has received critical acclaim for her performances in the series. She has also recently crossed over into the new *Doctor Who* series, garnering even more attention from her fans.

Maisie is a diminutive of Margaret, which was derived from Margarita, meaning "pearl" in Greek.

7. Natasha

Natasha Romanova ranks as one of the toughest women currently in the Avengers franchise. She proves time and time again that she doesn't need the fancy toys and powers that the other avengers rely on. She gets the job done through skill alone. Strong and independent, she doesn't hesitate to get her hands dirty when the situation calls for it.

Curiously enough, Natasha is the Russian derivation of "Christmas Day" in Latin. It also has an interestingly exotic sound to it as well.

8. Piper

Piper Chapmen, played by Taylor Schilling in *Orange is the New Black*, is a seemingly innocent character in this prison for women. However, as time goes on, it's slowly revealed that she has her own dark side, and that she will do what she must to get by. Despite this, she is still willing to reflect upon and work on the character flaws pointed out by her peers.

The name Piper stems from an English surname that was originally given to someone who played on a pipe.

Chapter 7: Old Names, New Spellings

Are you torn between wanting a unique name for your child and something a little more traditional? One trend is to choose a unique spelling of a common name. Certain letter-groups can be easily exchanged: *i* can become *y*, *y* can become *ie*, and *x* can become *cks*. However, you can also discover (and invent) a more experimental and dramatic name for your baby.

Unique Spellings of Common Boys' Names

Aaron	Aaren, Aarenn, Aarin, Aarinn, Aaryn, Aarynn, Aaronn
Alfred	Alphred, Allfred
Aldwin	Aldwyn, Alldwin, Aldwinn
Alex	Allex, Alecks
Austin	Austyn, Awstin, Austinn
Bailey	Baili, Baileigh, Baily, Bailee, Bailie, Bailei, Bayley, Bailley, Baeley, Bayley

Benjamin	Benjamyn, Bennjaminn
Brandon	Branden, Brandenn, Brandin, Brandinn, Brandyn, Brandynn, Branndonn
Brian	Bryan, Briann
Christopher	Kristopher, Krystopher, Krystofer, Kristofer, Christofer, Chrysofer, Chrystopher
Claude	Klaude, Cllaude, Clawde, Clode, Cloude
Danny	Danni, Danneigh, Danny, Dannee, Dannie, Danni, Danney, Dannie
Dominic	Dominik, Domynyc, Dominnic, Dominick
Dylon	Dilon, Dyllon, Dylen, Dylenn, Dylin, Dylinn, Dylyn, Dylynn, Dylonn
Eddie	Eddey, Eddee, Eddeigh, Eddi
Eric	Erick, Erik, Errik, Eryc
Griffin	Griphin, Gryffyn, Griffinn

Harry	Harri, Harreigh, Harry, Harree, Harrie, Harri
Jason	Jasen, Jasenn, Jasin, Jasinn, Jasyn, Jasynn, Jasonn, Jayson
Jessie	Jessey, Jessee, Jesseigh. Jessi
Johnny	Jonni, Jonneigh, Jonny, Jonnee, Jonnie, Jonni, Jonney, Jonnie
Jordan	Jordann, Jordin, Joardan, Jordyn, Jordayn,
Kevin	Cevin, Kevyn, Kevinn
Lawrence	Lawrense, Laurence, Lawrennce
Murphy	Murphi, Murpheigh, Murphy, Murphee, Murphie, Murfy, Murphi
Nicholas	Nikholas, Nycholasn Nichollas, Nnicholas
Oliver	Olyver, Olliver
Paul	Paull, Pawl

Preston	Presten, Prestenn, Prestin, Prestinn, Prestyn, Prestynn, Prestonn
Reggie	Reggey, Reggee, Reggeigh, Reggi
Riley	Rili, Rileigh. Rily, Rilee, Rilie, Rilei. Ryley, Rilley
Ryan	Rian, Ryann
Shaun	Shawn, Shaunn
Shayne	Shaine, Shaynne, Shaene, Shayne
Sinclair	Sinklair, Synclayr, Sincllair, Sinnclair, Sinclaer, Sinclayr
Terence	Terense, Terennce
Tyler	Tiler, Tyller

Unique Spellings of Common Girls' Names

Abigail	Abygayl, Abigaill, Abigael, Abigayl

Abby	Abbi, Abbeigh, Abby, Abbee, Abbie, Abbi
Addison	Addyson, Addisen, Addisenn, Addisin, Addisinn, Addisyn, Addisynn, Addisonn
Alex	Allex, Alecks
Allison	Alyson, Alisen, Alisenn, Alisin, Alisinn, Alisyn. Alisynn. Alisonn
Amelia	Aimelia, Aymelia, Amelya, Amellia
Ashley	Ashli, Ashleigh, Ashly, Ashlee, Ashlie, Ashlei, Ashlley
Betty	Betti, Betteigh, Bettee, Bettie, Betti
Brittany	Brittani, Brittaneigh, Brittany, Brittanee, Brittanie, Brittani, Brittaney, Brittanie, Bryttany, Brittanny
Caitlin	Kaitlin, Caytlyn, Caitllin, Caitlinn, Caetlin, Caytlin
Carla	Karla, Karlah, Kahrlah, Carlla, Carllah
Cindy	Cindi, Cindeigh, Cindy, Cindee, Cindie, Sindy, Cindi, Cyndy, Cinndy

Claire	Klaire, Cllaire, Claere, Clayre
Coraline	Koraline, Coralline, Coralinne, Coaraline
Courtney	Courtni, Courtneigh, Courtny, Courtnee, Courtnie, Kourtney, Courtnei, Courtnney
Elayne	Elaine, Ellayne, Elaynne, Elaene, Elayne
Eleanor	Elleanor, Eleannor, Eleanoar
Elizabeth	Elyzabeth, Ellizabeth, Elisabeth
Emily	Emili, Emileigh, Emily, Emilee, Emilie, Emili, Emyly, Emilly
Evelyn	Evelin, Evellyn, Evelynn
Gloria	Glorya, Glloria, Gloaria
Isabelle	Isabele, Izabelle
Jackie	Jaccie, Jakkie, Jakie, Jackey, Jackee, Jackeigh, Jacki
Jocelyn	Joselyn, Jocelin, Jocellyn, Jocelynn

Kirsty	Kirsti, Kirsteigh, Kirsty, Kirstee, Kirstie, Kirsty, Kirsti, Kyrsty
Layla	Laila, Laela, Layla
Lisa	Lysa, Liza
Madison	Madyson, Madisen, Madisenn, Madisin, Madisinn, Madisyn, Madisynn, Madisonn
Melissa	Melyssa, Mellissa, Melisza
Michaela	Mikhaela, Mychaela, Michaella, Michayla, Michaila
Nicole	Nikole, Nicolle, Nnicole
Natalie	Nataley, Natali, Nataly, Nataleigh, Natalee, Natallie, Nnatalie
Shannon	Shannen, Shannenn, Shannin, Shanninn, Shannyn, Shannynn
Sophie	Sofie, Sophey, Sophee, Sopheigh, Sophi
Tracy	Traci, Traceigh, Tracy, Tracee, Tracie, Trasey, Tracei

Victoria	Viktoria, Vyctorya, Victoaria
Zoe	Zoi, Zoeigh, Zoy, Zoee, Zoie, Zoei

Chapter 8: America's Top 100

The Top 50 Most Popular U.S. Boys' Names

Rank	Name	Origin	Meaning	Famous people
1	Noah	Hebrew	Rest; wandering	Noah Webster, Noah's Ark (Bible)
2	Liam	Irish	(Derived from William)	Liam Payne, Liam Neeson
3	Mason	English	Stoneworker	Mason Williams, George Mason
4	Jacob	Hebrew	Supplanter	Jacob Black (Twilight), Jacob Grimm, Jacob Lawrence
5	William	English (derived from German	Resolute Protection	William Shakespeare , Prince

		)		William
6	Ethan	Hebrew	Strong; firm	Ethan Hawke, Ethan Coen
7	Michael	Hebrew	Gift from God	Michael Jackson, George Michael
8	Alexander	Greek	People's defender	Alexander Graham Bell, Alexander Hamilton
9	James	Hebrew /English	(Derived from Jacob)	LeBron James, James Franco
10	Daniel	Hebrew	God is my judge	Daniel Radcliffe, Daniel Defoe
11	Elijah	Hebrew	Jehovah is God	Elijah Wood, Elijah the Prophet (Bible)
12	Benjamin	Hebrew	Son of the right hand	Benjamin King (Ben E. King), Benjamin

				Franklin
13	Logan	Scottish	From the hollow	Logan Butler, Logan Ryan
14	Aiden	Irish	Little fire; passionate	Aidan Quinn, Aiden (Beyond Two Souls)
15	Jayden	Hebrew	Thankful	Jaden Smith, Jayden Spears
16	Matthew	Hebrew	Gift of God	Matthew Morrison, Matthew McConaughey
17	Jackson	Scottish	God has been gracious	Jackson Pollock, Jackson Rathbone
18	David	Hebrew	Beloved	David Letterman, David (Bible – King of Israel)
19	Lucas	Hebrew /English	Light; luminous	George Lucas, Lucas

				Grabeel
20	Joseph	Hebrew	He will add (i.e. God will provide)	Joseph Gordon-Levitt, Joseph Haydn
21	Anthony	Latin	Priceless one; flower	Anthony Perkins, Anthony Hopkins
22	Andrew	Greek	Strong; masculine	Andrew Lloyd Webber, Andrew Jackson
23	Samuel	Hebrew	Heard by God	Samuel L. Jackson, Samuel Adams
24	Gabriel	Hebrew	God is my strength	Gabe Newell, Gabriel (Bible)
25	Joshua	Hebrew	The Lord is my salvation	Josh Hartnett, Josh Holloway
26	John	Hebrew	God is gracious	John Stamos,

				John D. Rockefeller
27	Carter	English	(occupational name) Transporter of goods by cart	Carter G. Woodson, Carter Smith
28	Luke	Greek	Short form of Lucas	Luke Bryan, Luke Perry, Luke Wilson
29	Dylan	Welsh	Son of the sea	Dylan Thomas, Dylan McDermott
30	Christop her	Greek	Bearer of Christ	Christopher Pratt, Christopher Walken, Christopher Reeve
31	Isaac	Hebrew	Laughter	Isaac Newton, Isaac Asimov
32	Oliver	Latin	Olive tree	Oliver Twist, Oliver Reed
33	Henry	German	Estate ruler	Henry Ford, Henry Winkler

34	Sebastian	Greek	Venerable; respected	Sebastian Stan, Sebastian Bach
35	Caleb	Hebrew	Devotion to God	Caleb Reynolds
36	Owen	Welsh	Young warrior; well-born	Owen Wilson, Owen Chamberlain
37	Ryan	Irish	Little king	Ryan Reynolds, Ryan Seacrest, Ryan Gosling
38	Nathan	Hebrew	Given	Nathan Fillion, Nathan Bedford Forrest
39	Wyatt	English (surname)	Brave in war	Wyatt Nash, Wyatt Earp
40	Hunter	English	One who hunts	Hunter Thompson, Hunter Hayes

41	Jack	English	God is gracious	Jack Nicholson, Jack White
42	Christian	Greek	Follower of Christ	Christian Bale, Christian Slater
43	Landon	English	Long hill	Landon Donovan, Landon Pigg
44	Jonathan	Hebrew	Gift of Jehovah	Jonathan Tunik, Jonathan Rhys Meyers
45	Levi	Hebrew	Joined; attached	Levi Strauss, Levi Coffin
46	Jaxon	Variation of Jackson	Son of Jack (English)	See Jackson
47	Julian	English	Youthful; downy	Julian Lennon, Julian Glover
48	Isaiah	Hebrew	Salvation of the Lord	Isaiah Mustafa, Isaiah Washington

49	Eli	Greek / Hebrew	Light / high	Eli Manning, Eli Wallach
50	Aaron	Hebrew / Arabic	Shining light; messenger	Aaron Carter

The Top 50 Most Popular U.S. Girl's Names

Rank	Name	Origin	Meaning	Famous people
1	Emma	German	All-Embracing	Emma Stone, Emma Thompson, Emma Watson
2	Olivia	French	Peace	Olivia Newton-John, Olivia Wilde
3	Sophia	Greek	Wisdom	Sophia Bush, Sophia Loren
4	Isabella	Spanish	Consecrated to God	Isabella Swan (Twilight),

				Isabella Rossellini
5	Ava	Latin	Blooming	Ava DuVernay, Ava Gardener
6	Mia	Scandinavian	Star of the sea	Mia Farrow, Mia Sara
7	Emily	Latin	Eager	Emily Robinson, Emily Dickinson
8	Abigail	Hebrew	A father's joy	Abigail Breslin, Abigail Adams
9	Madison	English	Good	Madison Riley
10	Charlotte	French	Petite; womanly	Princess Charlotte, Charlotte Brontë
11	Harper	Old Norse	Whaler	Harper Lee
12	Sofia	Greek	Wisdom	See Sophia
13	Avery	English	Counselor	

14	Elizabeth	Hebrew	God's oath; dedicated	Queen Elizabeth II, Elizabeth Taylor
15	Amelia	German	Industrious	Amelia Earhart, Amelia Boynton
16	Evelyn	English	Desired	Evelyn King, Evelyn Nesbit
17	Ella	German	Fairy maiden	Ella Fitzgerald, Ella Baker
18	Chloe	Greek	Fresh blooming	Chloe Bennett, Chloe Sevigny
19	Victoria	Latin	Victory	Victoria Beckham, Victoria Pratt
20	Aubrey	French	Fair ruler of the elves	Aubrey Plaza
21	Grace	English	Simple elegance	Grace Potter, Grace

				Gummer
22	Zoey	Greek	Life	Zooey Deschanel, Zoe Saldana
23	Natalie	Latin	Born at Christmas	Natalie Cole, Natalie Wood, Natalie Portman
24	Addison	Hebrew	Earth	Addison Timlin, Addison Powell
25	Lillian	Latin	(derived from Lily)	Lillian Gish
26	Brooklyn	Modern English	Beautiful brook	Brooklyn Sudano
27	Lily	Arabic	Of the night	Lily Allen, Lily Collins
28	Hannah	Hebrew	God is merciful; graceful one	Hannah Kearney, Hannah Murray
29	Layla	African	Dark beauty;	

			night	
30	Scarlett	Middle English	Deep red	Scarlett Pomers, Scarlett Johansson
31	Aria	German	Melody	Aria Curzon
32	Zoe	Greek	Life	Zoe Saldana
33	Samantha	Aramaic	Listens well	Samantha Eggar, Samantha Morton
34	Anna	Dutch	Bringer of peace/hope	Anna Faris, Anna Paquin, Anna Chlumsky
35	Leah	Hebrew	Wary	Leah Remini, Leah Pipes
36	Audrey	Old English	Noble Strength	Audrey Hepburn
37	Ariana	Hebrew	Like a beautiful melody	Ariana Grande
38	Allison	Irish	Of noble	Allison

			birth	Schmitt, Allison Janney
39	Savannah	Spanish	A type of biome	Savannah Outen
40	Arianna	Hebrew	See Ariana	See Ariana
41	Camila	Latin	Free-born; noble	Camila Alves
42	Penelope	Greek	Bobbin; a weaver	Penelope Cruz
43	Gabriella	Hebrew	See Gabriel	Gabriella Wilde
44	Claire	Latin	Bright	Claire Danes
45	Aaliyah	Hebrew	Exalted; extreme happiness	Aaliyah (Houghton)
46	Sadie	English	Princess	Sadie Frost
47	Riley	Irish	Courageous	Riley Keough
48	Skylar	Dutch	Scholar	Skylar Grey
49	Nora	Greek	Light	Nora Roberts, Nora

				Ephron
50	Sarah	Hebrew	Princess	Sarah Silverman, Sarah Michelle Gellar

Chapter 9: Index of Over 2000 Boys' Names

A

1. Aaden
2. Aaran
3. Aarav
4. Aaren
5. Aaron
6. Ab
7. Abbot
8. Abbott
9. Abdiel
10. Abdullah
11. Abe
12. Abel
13. Abell
14. Abia
15. Abiah
16. Abida
17. Abidah
18. Abidan
19. Abiel
20. Abihail
21. Abihu
22. Abijah
23. Abiram
24. Able
25. Abnar
26. Abner
27. Abnor
28. Abnur
29. Abot
30. Abott
31. Abraham
32. Abram
33. Absalom
34. Ace
35. Acer
36. Acey
37. Achan
38. Achar
39. Acie
40. Acke
41. Acker
42. Ackerlea
43. Ackerley
44. Ackerly
45. Acklea
46. Ackley
47. Acklie
48. Acton
49. Adalia
50. Adaliah
51. Adam
52. Adan
53. Adare
54. Addam
55. Addison
56. Aden

57. Adeno
58. Adin
59. Adina
60. Adino
61. Adison
62. Adisson
63. Adlai
64. Adney
65. Adolph
66. Adonia
67. Adonis
68. Adrian
69. Adriel
70. Adrien
71. Aengus
72. Affton
73. Afton
74. Agustin
75. Ahab
76. Ahern
77. Ahearn
78. Aherin
79. Aherne
80. Ahmad
81. Ahmed
82. Aidan
83. Aiden
84. Aidyn
85. Aillard
86. Ailward
87. Aimery
88. Al
89. Aladdin
90. Alan
91. Alann
92. Alban
93. Albert
94. Alberto
95. Albin
96. Alby
97. Alden
98. Aldo
99. Aldford
100. Aldin
101. Aldine
102. Alduous
103. Aldred
104. Aldrich
105. Aldridge
106. Aldus
107. Aldwen
108. Aldwin
109. Alec
110. Aleck
111. Alejandro
112. Alen
113. Aleric
114. Alerick
115. Alessandro
116. Alex
117. Alexander
118. Alexis
119. Alexzander
120. Alf
121. Alfie
122. Alfonso
123. Alfonzo
124. Alford
125. Alfred
126. Alfredo

127. Alfrid
128. Alfy
129. Algar
130. Alger
131. Algernon
132. Ali
133. Alic
134. Alick
135. Alijah
136. Alik
137. Alix
138. Allan
139. Allard
140. Allaric
141. Allarick
142. Allaster
143. Allastir
144. Allen
145. Alleric
146. Allerick
147. Allgar
148. Allger
149. Allin
150. Allistair
151. Allister
152. Allistir
153. Allon
154. Allric
155. Allyn
156. Allysdair
157. Allysdare
158. Allystair
159. Allyster
160. Alon
161. Alonso
162. Alonzo
163. Alpha
164. Alphonzo
165. Alpin
166. Alpine
167. Altair
168. Alton
169. Allured
170. Alvar
171. Alvaro
172. Alven
173. Alive
174. Alvin
175. Alvred
176. Alvy
177. Alvyn
178. Alwin
179. Alwyn
180. Alysdair
181. Alysdare
182. Alyster
183. Alystair
184. Amare
185. Amari
186. Amaria
187. Amariah
188. Amasai
189. Ambie
190. Ambrose
191. Amby
192. Ameer
193. Amery
194. Ami
195. Amir
196. Amitai

197. Amittai
198. Ammiel
199. Ammon
200. Amon
201. Amory
202. Amos
203. Amoz
204. Amran
205. Anakin
206. Anani
207. Ananiah
208. Ananias
209. Anders
210. Anderson
211. Andre
212. Andres
213. Andrew
214. Andy
215. Angel
216. Angelo
217. Angus
218. Anson
219. Anthony
220. Anton
221. Antony
222. Antonio
223. Antuan
224. Antwan
225. Apollo
226. Archer
227. Archibald
228. Archie
229. Ardal
230. Arden
231. Ardon
232. Areli
233. Ares
234. Ari
235. Arian
236. Aric
237. Arieh
238. Ariel
239. Arik
240. Arin
241. Arjun
242. Arley
243. Arlie
244. Arlo
245. Armando
246. Armani
247. Arn
248. Arnav
249. Arne
250. Arnie
251. Arnold
252. Arny
253. Aron
254. Arran
255. Arron
256. Arryn
257. Art
258. Arthur
259. Artie
260. Artur
261. Arturo
262. Arvin
263. Aryan
264. Asa
265. Asaf
266. Asaph

267. Asareel
268. Ash
269. Asher
270. Ashley
271. Ashriel
272. Ashton
273. Ashur
274. Asia
275. Asshur
276. Assur
277. Aston
278. Astrophel
279. Atlas
280. Atticus
281. Aubrey
282. Aubry
283. Aubyn
284. Audley
285. August
286. Augustine
287. Augustus
288. Aulay
289. Austen
290. Austin
291. Austyn
292. Autumn
293. Averel
294. Averill
295. Avery
296. Avon
297. Axel
298. Axl
299. Axton
300. Ayaan
301. Ayan
302. Aydan
303. Ayden
304. Aydin
305. Aylmer
306. Aylward
307. Aymery
308. Azal
309. Azaniah
310. Azarael
311. Azareel
312. Azariah
313. Azazel
314. Azel
315. Azrael
316. Azriel
317. Azuriah

B

---

318. Babe
319. Bailey
320. Bailie
321. Baily
322. Baldwin
323. Ballard
324. Balthasar
325. Balthazar
326. Bani
327. Baptist
328. Barnaby
329. Barney
330. Barret
331. Barrett
332. Barrie

333. Barry
334. Bart
335. Bartholomew
336. Bartlet
337. Bartley
338. Baruch
339. Bas
340. Basil
341. Bassett
342. Bastian
343. Baxter
344. Baylor
345. Baz
346. Beavis
347. Beau
348. Beckett
349. Beckham
350. Bedivere
351. Ben
352. Benedict
353. Benet
354. Benett
355. Benjamin
356. Benji
357. Benjie
358. Benjy
359. Bennet
360. Bennett
361. Bennie
362. Benny
363. Benson
364. Bentlee
365. Bentley
366. Benton
367. Berkeley
368. Bernard
369. Bernie
370. Berry
371. Bert
372. Bertie
373. Beverley
374. Bevis
375. Biff
376. Bill
377. Billy
378. Blaine
379. Blaise
380. Blaize
381. Blake
382. Blaze
383. Bliss
384. Blithe
385. Bo
386. Boaz
387. Bob
388. Bobbi
389. Bobby
390. Bode
391. Boden
392. Bodhi
393. Bodie
394. Booker
395. Boston
396. Bowen
397. Brad
398. Bradburn
399. Braden
400. Bradford
401. Bradley
402. Brady

403. Braeden
404. Braiden
405. Braidy
406. Bran
407. Branden
408. Brandon
409. Brandt
410. Brannon
411. Branson
412. Brant
413. Brantlee
414. Brantley
415. Braxton
416. Brayan
417. Brayden
418. Braydon
419. Braylen
420. Braylon
421. Brayson
422. Brecken
423. Brendan
424. Brenden
425. Brendon
426. Brennan
427. Brent
428. Brentley
429. Brenton
430. Bret
431. Brett
432. Brian
433. Briar
434. Brigham
435. Brice
436. Bridger
437. Briggs
438. Briscoe
439. Britton
440. Brock
441. Broderick
442. Brodie
443. Brody
444. Bronson
445. Brook
446. Brooke
447. Brooks
448. Brose
449. Bruce
450. Bruno
451. Brutus
452. Bryan
453. Bryant
454. Bryce
455. Brycen
456. Bryon
457. Bryson
458. Buck
459. Bud
460. Buddy
461. Burney
462. Burt
463. Burton
464. Buster
465. Butch
466. Buz
467. Byrne
468. Byron
469. Bysshe

C

470. Cade
471. Caden
472. Cadence
473. Caiden
474. Cain
475. Cainan
476. Cairo
477. Cal
478. Calder
479. Cale
480. Caleb
481. Callan
482. Callen
483. Callum
484. Calvert
485. Calvin
486. Cam
487. Camden
488. Camdyn
489. Cameron
490. Camilo
491. Camp
492. Campion
493. Camren
494. Camron
495. Canan
496. Cannon
497. Carbrey
498. Carbry
499. Carey
500. Cari
501. Carl
502. Carlisle
503. Carlton
504. Carlos
505. Carlyle
506. Carmelo
507. Carmi
508. Carran
509. Carrol
510. Carroll
511. Carson
512. Carter
513. Carver
514. Cary
515. Case
516. Casey
517. Casen
518. Casey
519. Cash
520. Casimir
521. Cason
522. Casper
523. Cassidy
524. Cassius
525. Castiel
526. Catigern
527. Cayden
528. Cayson
529. Cecil
530. Cedric
531. Cenric
532. Cesar
533. Chace
534. Chad
535. Chadwick
536. Chaim
537. Chance
538. Chandler
539. Channing

540. Charles
541. Charley
542. Charlie
543. Charlton
544. Chas
545. Chase
546. Chauncey
547. Chauncy
548. Chaz
549. Chenaniah
550. Cherokee
551. Chesed
552. Chester
553. Chet
554. Chevy
555. Cheyanne
556. Cheyenne
557. Chip
558. Chris
559. Christian
560. Christopher
561. Chuck
562. Chuckie
563. Clancey
564. Clancy
565. Clare
566. Clarence
567. Clark
568. Clarke
569. Claud
570. Claude
571. Clay
572. Clayton
573. Clem
574. Clement
575. Clements
576. Clemmie
577. Cletis
578. Cletus
579. Cleve
580. Cleveland
581. Cliff
582. Clifford
583. Clifton
584. Clint
585. Clinton
586. Clive
587. Clyde
588. Codie
589. Cody
590. Coen
591. Cohen
592. Colbert
593. Colby
594. Cole
595. Coleman
596. Colin
597. Collin
598. Colm
599. Colman
600. Colt
601. Colten
602. Colton
603. Conan
604. Conley
605. Connell
606. Conner
607. Connor
608. Conor
609. Conrad

610. Constantine
611. Conway
612. Cooper
613. Corbin
614. Cordell
615. Corey
616. Cori
617. Corie
618. Cornelius
619. Cort
620. Cortney
621. Cory
622. Coty
623. Courtney
624. Cowal
625. Craig
626. Craige
627. Crawford
628. Crew
629. Crispian
630. Crispin
631. Cristian
632. Cristiano
633. Cristopher
634. Crofton
635. Crosby
636. Cruz
637. Cullen
638. Curi
639. Curtis
640. Cush
641. Cuthbert
642. Cy
643. Cymbeline
644. Cyril
645. Cyrus

D

---

646. Dacey
647. Dakota
648. Dale
649. Daley
650. Dallas
651. Dalton
652. Daly
653. Damari
654. Damian
655. Damien
656. Damion
657. Damon
658. Dan
659. Dane
660. Daniel
661. Danni
662. Dannie
663. Danny
664. Dante
665. Darby
666. Darcie
667. Darcy
668. Darden
669. Darell
670. Daren
671. Darian
672. Dariel
673. Darien
674. Darin
675. Dario

676. Darius
677. Darnell
678. Darrel
679. Darrell
680. Darren
681. Darrin
682. Darryl
683. Darwin
684. Daryl
685. Dash
686. Dashiell
687. Dave
688. Daven
689. Davey
690. Davian
691. David
692. Davin
693. Davion
694. Davis
695. Davy
696. Daw
697. Dawson
698. Dax
699. Daxton
700. Daye
701. Dayton
702. Deacon
703. Dean
704. Deandre
705. Deangelo
706. Declan
707. Dee
708. Deemer
709. Deforest
710. Deforrest
711. Delaia
712. Delaiah
713. Delaney
714. Delbert
715. Dell
716. Delmar
717. Delroy
718. Demetrius
719. Deming
720. Den
721. Dene
722. Denis
723. Dennis
724. Denny
725. Denton
726. Denver
727. Denys
728. Deon
729. Deonne
730. Deonte
731. Derby
732. Derek
733. Derick
734. Dermot
735. Derren
736. Derrick
737. Derry
738. Derryl
739. Derwin
740. Deryck
741. Deshaun
742. Deshawn
743. Desmond
744. Devan
745. Deven

746. Devereux
747. Devin
748. Devon
749. Dewayne
750. Dewey
751. Dexter
752. Deye
753. Dezi
754. Dhelweard
755. Dibri
756. Dick
757. Dickie
758. Dicky
759. Diego
760. Digby
761. Diggory
762. Digory
763. Dikla
764. Diklah
765. Dilan
766. Dilbert
767. Dillon
768. Dimitri
769. Dinis
770. Dishan
771. Dismas
772. Dob
773. Dodge
774. Dolphe
775. Dom
776. Domenic
777. Dominic
778. Dominick
779. Dominik
780. Dominique
781. Don
782. Donaghy
783. Donal
784. Donald
785. Donall
786. Donnie
787. Donny
788. Donogh
789. Donough
790. Donovan
791. Doran
792. Dore
793. Dorian
794. Doug
795. Dougal
796. Dougie
797. Douglas
798. Doyle
799. Drake
800. Draven
801. Drew
802. Driscoll
803. Driskoll
804. Duane
805. Dud
806. Dudda
807. Dudde
808. Dudley
809. Duff
810. Duffy
811. Dugal
812. Duke
813. Duncan
814. Dunky
815. Dunn

816. Durward
817. Dustin
818. Dusty
819. Dwane
820. Dwayne
821. Dwight
822. Dye
823. Dyl
824. Dylan
825. Dyson

E

826. Eade
827. Eamon
828. Ean
829. Earl
830. Earle
831. Earnest
832. Earnie
833. Eason
834. Easter
835. Easton
836. Eb
837. Ebbie
838. Ebby
839. Ebenezer
840. Eber
841. Ed
842. Edan
843. Eddie
844. Eddy
845. Eden
846. Edgar
847. Edison
848. Edmund
849. Edric
850. Edson
851. Eduardo
852. Edun
853. Edward
854. Edwin
855. Edwyn
856. Efrain
857. Egbert
858. Elada
859. Eladah
860. Elam
861. Elbert
862. Elbie
863. Elbridge
864. Elden
865. Eldin
866. Eldis
867. Eldon
868. Eldous
869. Eldred
870. Eldridge
871. Eldwen
872. Eldwin
873. Eleazar
874. Elgar
875. Elger
876. Elhanan
877. Eli
878. Eliab
879. Eliah
880. Elian
881. Elias

882. Eliezer
883. Elijah
884. Eliot
885. Eliott
886. Eliseo
887. Elisha
888. Ella
889. Ellery
890. Ellgar
891. Ellger
892. Elliot
893. Elliott
894. Ellis
895. Elmer
896. Elpalet
897. Elric
898. Elrod
899. Elrond
900. Elroy
901. Elsdon
902. Elton
903. Elvin
904. Elvis
905. Elweard
906. Elwin
907. Elwood
908. Elwyn
909. Emanuel
910. Emerson
911. Emery
912. Emil
913. Emiliano
914. Emilio
915. Emmanuel
916. Emmerson
917. Emmet
918. Emmett
919. Emmitt
920. Emory
921. Enda
922. Enoch
923. Enos
924. Enosh
925. Enrique
926. Enzo
927. Ephah
928. Ephraim
929. Erek
930. Eric
931. Erick
932. Erik
933. Erle
934. Ern
935. Ernest
936. Ernesto
937. Ernie
938. Errol
939. Erroll
940. Ervin
941. Erwin
942. Eryk
943. Esmond
944. Esmund
945. Esteban
946. Estmond
947. Estmund
948. Ethan
949. Euan
950. Eugene
951. Euseby

952. Eustace
953. Evan
954. Evelyn
955. Everett
956. Everitt
957. Ewain
958. Ewan
959. Ewane
960. Ewen
961. Ezekiel
962. Ezequiel
963. Ezra

F

---

964. Fabian
965. Farley
966. Faron
967. Farran
968. Farrell
969. Fawke
970. Felim
971. Felipe
972. Felis
973. Felix
974. Felyse
975. Fenton
976. Ferd
977. Ferdie
978. Ferdinand
979. Ferdy
980. Fergal
981. Fergie
982. Fergus
983. Fernando
984. Fester
985. Festus
986. Fido
987. Filander
988. Filbert
989. Fillin
990. Finbar
991. Findlay
992. Fingal
993. Fingall
994. Finian
995. Finlay
996. Finley
997. Finn
998. Finnegan
999. Finnian
1000. Finnley
1001. Fintan
1002. Fisher
1003. Flannery
1004. Fletcher
1005. Flint
1006. Florence
1007. Florry
1008. Flurry
1009. Flynn
1010. Foley
1011. Fonz
1012. Fonzie
1013. Ford
1014. Forest
1015. Forrest
1016. Foster
1017. Fowke

1018. Fox
1019. France
1020. Francis
1021. Francisco
1022. Franco
1023. Frank
1024. Frankie
1025. Franklin
1026. Franklyn
1027. Fraser
1028. Frazer
1029. Frazier
1030. Fred
1031. Freddie
1032. Freddy
1033. Frederick
1034. Fredric
1035. Fredrick
1036. Fredrik
1037. Freeman
1038. Fulk
1039. Fulke

G

1040. Gabby
1041. Gabe
1042. Gable
1043. Gabriel
1044. Gaddiel
1045. Gadiel
1046. Gael
1047. Gage
1048. Gaige
1049. Gail
1050. Gair
1051. Galahad
1052. Gale
1053. Galen
1054. Galilee
1055. Gallagher
1056. Gamaliel
1057. Gamliel
1058. Gannon
1059. Gare
1060. Gareth
1061. Garey
1062. Garfield
1063. Garland
1064. Garnet
1065. Garnett
1066. Garret
1067. Garrett
1068. Garrick
1069. Garth
1070. Garvan
1071. Gary
1072. Gauge
1073. Gavin
1074. Gavyn
1075. Gawain
1076. Gayelord
1077. Gaylon
1078. Gaylord
1079. Gaynor
1080. Gearalt
1081. Ged
1082. Gedalia
1083. Gedaliah

1084. Geffrey
1085. Gemariah
1086. Gemini
1087. Gene
1088. Geoff
1089. Geoffrey
1090. Geordie
1091. George
1092. Georgie
1093. Gerald
1094. Gerard
1095. Gerardo
1096. Gerrard
1097. Gerry
1098. Gershom
1099. Gershon
1100. Gervase
1101. Giancarlo
1102. Gianni
1103. Gib
1104. Gibson
1105. Gideon
1106. Gifard
1107. Giffard
1108. Gil
1109. Gilbert
1110. Gilead
1111. Giles
1112. Gilford
1113. Gill
1114. Gillespie
1115. Gilroy
1116. Gino
1117. Giovani
1118. Giovanni
1119. Giovanny
1120. Gladwin
1121. Gladwyn
1122. Glen
1123. Glendower
1124. Glenn
1125. Goddard
1126. Godfrey
1127. Gog
1128. Golda
1129. Goliath
1130. Gomer
1131. Goodwin
1132. Gord
1133. Gorden
1134. Gordon
1135. Grady
1136. Graham
1137. Grant
1138. Granville
1139. Gray
1140. Graysen
1141. Grayson
1142. Greer
1143. Greg
1144. Gregg
1145. Gregory
1146. Grenville
1147. Grey
1148. Greyson
1149. Grier
1150. Griffin
1151. Griffith
1152. Grover
1153. Guillero

1154. Gunnar
1155. Gunner
1156. Gus
1157. Gustavo
1158. Guy
1159. Gyles

H

1160. Hadad
1161. Hadley
1162. Hadwin
1163. Hagai
1164. Haggai
1165. Haggi
1166. Haig
1167. Hal
1168. Hale
1169. Hall
1170. Ham
1171. Hamilton
1172. Hamish
1173. Hamlet
1174. Hammond
1175. Hamuel
1176. Hamza
1177. Hanael
1178. Hanan
1179. Hanani
1180. Haniel
1181. Hank
1182. Hanley
1183. Harcourt
1184. Harding
1185. Hardy
1186. Harlan
1187. Harland
1188. Harley
1189. Harlin
1190. Harmon
1191. Harold
1192. Harper
1193. Harri
1194. Harrie
1195. Harris
1196. Harrison
1197. Harry
1198. Hartley
1199. Harve
1200. Harvey
1201. Harvie
1202. Hassan
1203. Havelock
1204. Haven
1205. Haward
1206. Hayden
1207. Hayes
1208. Haywood
1209. Headley
1210. Heath
1211. Heathcliff
1212. Heber
1213. Heck
1214. Hector
1215. Hedley
1216. Hengist
1217. Hendrix
1218. Henrie
1219. Henrik

1220. Henry
1221. Henrye
1222. Herb
1223. Herbie
1224. Herk
1225. Herman
1226. Heron
1227. Hervey
1228. Hewie
1229. Hezekiah
1230. Hiel
1231. Hilary
1232. Hillary
1233. Hirah
1234. Hiram
1235. Hodge
1236. Holden
1237. Hollis
1238. Hopkin
1239. Horace
1240. Horatio
1241. Horsa
1242. Houston
1243. Howard
1244. Howel
1245. Howell
1246. Howie
1247. Hoyt
1248. Hudson
1249. Hue
1250. Huey
1251. Huet
1252. Huffie
1253. Hugh
1254. Hughe
1255. Hughie
1256. Hugo
1257. Hum
1258. Humbert
1259. Humphrey
1260. Humphry
1261. Hunter
1262. Huntley
1263. Huxley
1264. Hiram
1265. Hyram

I

1266. Ian
1267. Ibrahim
1268. Ibri
1269. Ichabod
1270. Ignatius
1271. Ike
1272. Iker
1273. Imanuel
1274. Imla
1275. Imlah
1276. Immanuel
1277. Imri
1278. Indiana
1279. Indigo
1280. Indy
1281. Ingram
1282. Innes

1283. Innocent
1284. Ira
1285. Irvin
1286. Irvine
1287. Irving
1288. Irwin
1289. Isa
1290. Isaac
1291. Isador
1292. Isadore
1293. Isaiah
1294. Isaias
1295. Ishaan
1296. Ishmael
1297. Isiah
1298. Isidore
1299. Ismael
1300. Israel
1301. Issac
1302. Ivan
1303. Ivo
1304. Izaiah
1305. Izzy

J

1306. Jabez
1307. Jabin
1308. Jace
1309. Jack
1310. Jackie
1311. Jackson
1312. Jacob
1313. Jacoby
1314. Jada
1315. Jade
1316. Jaden
1317. Jadiel
1318. Jadon
1319. Jadyn
1320. Jae
1321. Jafet
1322. Jagger
1323. Jahleel
1324. Jahzeel
1325. Jai
1326. Jaiden
1327. Jaime
1328. Jaimie
1329. Jair
1330. Jairo
1331. Jairus
1332. Jake
1333. Jakob
1334. Jalen
1335. Jalon
1336. Jamal
1337. Jamar
1338. Jamari
1339. Jamarion
1340. James
1341. Jameson
1342. Jamey
1343. Jamie
1344. Jamieson
1345. Jamin
1346. Jamir
1347. Jamison
1348. Jan

1349. Jankin
1350. Japeth
1351. Japhet
1352. Japheth
1353. Jareb
1354. Jared
1355. Jareth
1356. Jarod
1357. Jaron
1358. Jarred
1359. Jarrett
1360. Jarrod
1361. Jarvis
1362. Jase
1363. Jashub
1364. Jasiah
1365. Jason
1366. Jasper
1367. Javan
1368. Javier
1369. Javion
1370. Javon
1371. Jax
1372. Jaxen
1373. Jaxon
1374. Jaxson
1375. Jaxton
1376. Jay
1377. Jayce
1378. Jayceon
1379. Jaycob
1380. Jayden
1381. Jaydon
1382. Jaye
1383. Jaylen
1384. Jaylin
1385. Jaylon
1386. Jaylyn
1387. Jaymes
1388. Jayse
1389. Jayson
1390. Jayvion
1391. Jeb
1392. Jed
1393. Jedidiah
1394. Jeff
1395. Jefferson
1396. Jeffery
1397. Jeffrey
1398. Jeffry
1399. Jehiel
1400. Jehoash
1401. Jehohanan
1402. Jehoram
1403. Jehosaphat
1404. Jehoshua
1405. Jehu
1406. Jehudi
1407. Jem
1408. Jimmy
1409. Jenkin
1410. Jensen
1411. Jep
1412. Jephtha
1413. Jeptha
1414. Jerald
1415. Jere
1416. Jered
1417. Jeremiah
1418. Jeremiel

1419. Jeremy
1420. Jeriah
1421. Jericho
1422. Jermaine
1423. Jerold
1424. Jerome
1425. Jerrard
1426. Jerred
1427. Jerrod
1428. Jerrold
1429. Jerry
1430. Jervis
1431. Jesaiah
1432. Jeshua
1433. Jess
1434. Jesse
1435. Jessie
1436. Jesus
1437. Jether
1438. Jethro
1439. Jett
1440. Jim
1441. Jimi
1442. Jimmie
1443. Jimmy
1444. Jo
1445. Joab
1446. Joah
1447. Joahaz
1448. Joash
1449. Joaquin
1450. Job
1451. Joby
1452. Jocelyn
1453. Jock
1454. Jody
1455. Joe
1456. Joel
1457. Joey
1458. Johan
1459. Johanan
1460. John
1461. Johnathan
1462. Johnathon
1463. Johnie
1464. Johnnie
1465. Johnny
1466. Jojo
1467. Joktan
1468. Jolyon
1469. Jon
1470. Jona
1471. Jonah
1472. Jonas
1473. Jonathan
1474. Jonathon
1475. Jonny
1476. Jonty
1477. Jools
1478. Jophiel
1479. Joram
1480. Jordan
1481. Jordi
1482. Jordie
1483. Jordon
1484. Jordy
1485. Jordyn
1486. Jorge
1487. Josaphat
1488. Jose

1489. Joseph
1490. Joses
1491. Josh
1492. Joshawa
1493. Joshua
1494. Josiah
1495. Joss
1496. Josse
1497. Josue
1498. Jotham
1499. Jovani
1500. Jovanni
1501. Joyce
1502. Joziah
1503. Juan
1504. Juda
1505. Judah
1506. Judd
1507. Jude
1508. Judson
1509. Jules
1510. Julian
1511. Julien
1512. Julyan
1513. Julio
1514. Julius
1515. Junior
1516. Justice
1517. Justin
1518. Justus
1519. Justy

K

1520. Kade
1521. Kaden
1522. Kae
1523. Kaeden
1524. Kai
1525. Kaiden
1526. Kaison
1527. Kale
1528. Kaleb
1529. Kalel
1530. Kam
1531. Kamari
1532. Kamden
1533. Kamdyn
1534. Kameron
1535. Kamron
1536. Kamryn
1537. Kane
1538. Kannon
1539. Kaolin
1540. Kareem
1541. Karson
1542. Karter
1543. Kase
1544. Kasen
1545. Kasey
1546. Kash
1547. Kason
1548. Kasper
1549. Kassidy
1550. Kay
1551. Kayden

1552. Kaysen
1553. Kayson
1554. Keagan
1555. Kean
1556. Keane
1557. Kearney
1558. Keaton
1559. Keefe
1560. Keegan
1561. Keelan
1562. Keelin
1563. Keenan
1564. Kegan
1565. Keir
1566. Keith
1567. Kelan
1568. Kelcey
1569. Kell
1570. Kellan
1571. Kellen
1572. Kelley
1573. Kelly
1574. Kelsey
1575. Kelvin
1576. Kemp
1577. Ken
1578. Kenan
1579. Kendal
1580. Kendall
1581. Kendrick
1582. Kenelm
1583. Kenith
1584. Kennard
1585. Kennedy
1586. Kenneth
1587. Kenny
1588. Kenrick
1589. Kent
1590. Kenton
1591. Kenyon
1592. Kenzie
1593. Kermit
1594. Kerr
1595. Kerrie
1596. Kerry
1597. Keshaun
1598. Keshawn
1599. Kevan
1600. Kevin
1601. Kevyn
1602. Khalid
1603. Khalil
1604. Kian
1605. Kiaran
1606. Kieran
1607. Killeen
1608. Killian
1609. Kim
1610. Kimball
1611. Kimbell
1612. King
1613. Kingsley
1614. Kingston
1615. Kip
1616. Kipp
1617. Kirby
1618. Kirk
1619. Kit
1620. Knox
1621. Kobe

1622. Kodey
1623. Kody
1624. Koen
1625. Kohen
1626. Kolby
1627. Kole
1628. Kolman
1629. Kolten
1630. Kolton
1631. Konner
1632. Konnor
1633. Korah
1634. Korbin
1635. Korey
1636. Kori
1637. Kortney
1638. Kris
1639. Kristian
1640. Kristopher
1641. Kurt
1642. Kurtis
1643. Kylan
1644. Kyle
1645. Kylen
1646. Kyler
1647. Kymani
1648. Kyran
1649. Kyree
1650. Kyrie
1651. Kyson

L

1652. Lachlan
1653. Lake
1654. Lamar
1655. Lambart
1656. Lambert
1657. Lamont
1658. Lance
1659. Landen
1660. Landon
1661. Landry
1662. Landyn
1663. Lane
1664. Lanford
1665. Langdon
1666. Langston
1667. Lanny
1668. Lark
1669. Larkin
1670. Larrie
1671. Larry
1672. Lauren
1673. Laurence
1674. Laurie
1675. Lavern
1676. Laverne
1677. Law
1678. Lawrence
1679. Lawrie
1680. Lawson
1681. Layne
1682. Layton
1683. Laz

1684. Leandro
1685. Lee
1686. Leeroy
1687. Legend
1688. Leif
1689. Leighton
1690. Leland
1691. Lem
1692. Lemual
1693. Len
1694. Lenard
1695. Lennard
1696. Lennie
1697. Lennon
1698. Lennox
1699. Lenny
1700. Leo
1701. Leolin
1702. Leon
1703. Leonard
1704. Leonardo
1705. Leonel
1706. Leonidas
1707. Leopold
1708. Leroi
1709. Leroy
1710. Les
1711. Lesley
1712. Lesly
1713. Lester
1714. Lev
1715. Levi
1716. Lew
1717. Lewin
1718. Lewis
1719. Lex
1720. Leyton
1721. Liam
1722. Lincoln
1723. Linden
1724. Lindon
1725. Lindsay
1726. Lindsey
1727. Linford
1728. Linton
1729. Linus
1730. Lionel
1731. Livy
1732. Lloyd
1733. Lochlan
1734. Logan
1735. Lon
1736. London
1737. Lonnie
1738. Lonny
1739. Loren
1740. Lorenzo
1741. Lorin
1742. Lorn
1743. Lorne
1744. Lorrin
1745. Lou
1746. Louie
1747. Louis
1748. Lovel
1749. Lovell
1750. Lowell
1751. Loyd
1752. Luca
1753. Lucas

1754. Lucca
1755. Lucian
1756. Luciano
1757. Luis
1758. Luka
1759. Lukas
1760. Luke
1761. Luther
1762. Lux
1763. Lyle
1764. Lyndon
1765. Lynton
1766. Lyric
1767. Lysander

M

1768. Mace
1769. Macey
1770. Macie
1771. Mack
1772. Mackenzie
1773. Macy
1774. Madai
1775. Madden
1776. Maddison
1777. Maddox
1778. Maddux
1779. Madison
1780. Magnus
1781. Mahala
1782. Mahalah
1783. Mahli
1784. Mahlon
1785. Mahon
1786. Maison
1787. Maitland
1788. Major
1789. Makai
1790. Makhi
1791. Malach
1792. Malachai
1793. Malachi
1794. Malachy
1795. Malakai
1796. Malcolm
1797. Malcom
1798. Malik
1799. Mallory
1800. Malone
1801. Manley
1802. Mannix
1803. Manuel
1804. Manny
1805. Marc
1806. Marcel
1807. Marcelo
1808. March
1809. Marco
1810. Marcos
1811. Marcus
1812. Mario
1813. Mark
1814. Marko
1815. Markus
1816. Marlen
1817. Marlin
1818. Marley
1819. Marlon

1820. Marlowe
1821. Marmaduke
1822. Marquis
1823. Marquise
1824. Marshal
1825. Marshall
1826. Martial
1827. Martie
1828. Martin
1829. Marty
1830. Marvin
1831. Marvyn
1832. Mason
1833. Mat
1834. Matania
1835. Mateo
1836. Mathew
1837. Mathias
1838. Matias
1839. Matt
1840. Matteo
1841. Matthew
1842. Matthias
1843. Mattie
1844. Matty
1845. Maurice
1846. Mauricio
1847. Maverick
1848. Max
1849. Maxim
1850. Maximilian
1851. Maximiliano
1852. Maximo
1853. Maximus
1854. Maxton
1855. Maxwell
1856. Maynard
1857. Maynerd
1858. Mayson
1859. Mckenzie
1860. Mead
1861. Meade
1862. Meedad
1863. Meed
1864. Mekhi
1865. Mel
1866. Melbourne
1867. Melech
1868. Melville
1869. Melvin
1870. Melvyn
1871. Melvin
1872. Memphis
1873. Meredith
1874. Merit
1875. Merle
1876. Merlin
1877. Merlyn
1878. Merrick
1879. Merrill
1880. Merritt
1881. Merton
1882. Merv
1883. Mervin
1884. Mervyn
1885. Meryl
1886. Meryle
1887. Messiah
1888. Micah
1889. Micaiah

1890. Micha
1891. Michael
1892. Michaya
1893. Micheal
1894. Mick
1895. Mickey
1896. MIcky
1897. Midian
1898. Miguel
1899. Mike
1900. Miki
1901. Milan
1902. Milburn
1903. Mile
1904. Miles
1905. Milford
1906. Millard
1907. Miller
1908. Milo
1909. Milton
1910. Misael
1911. Mitch
1912. Mitchell
1913. Miykah
1914. Mo
1915. Moab
1916. Moe
1917. Mohamed
1918. Mohammad
1919. Mohammed
1920. Moise
1921. Moises
1922. Montague
1923. Monte
1924. Montgomery
1925. Monty
1926. Mordecai
1927. Mordechai
1928. Mordred
1929. Morgan
1930. Morgen
1931. Moriarty
1932. Morley
1933. Morris
1934. Morrissey
1935. Mort
1936. Mortimer
1937. Morton
1938. Morty
1939. Mose
1940. Moses
1941. Moshe
1942. Moss
1943. Muhammad
1944. Murdie
1945. Murdo
1946. Murdoch
1947. Murdock
1948. Murdy
1949. Murphy
1950. Murray
1951. Murtagh
1952. Murty
1953. Mustafa
1954. Myles
1955. Myron

N

1956. Naftali
1957. Nahor
1958. Nahum
1959. Nandy
1960. Naphtali
1961. Nash
1962. Nasir
1963. Nat
1964. Nathan
1965. Nathanael
1966. Nathaniel
1967. Neal
1968. Neas
1969. Ned
1970. Neely
1971. Nehemiah
1972. Neil
1973. Neill
1974. Nekoda
1975. Nelson
1976. Neo
1977. Nevada
1978. Nevan
1979. Nevil
1980. Neville
1981. Nevin
1982. Newt
1983. Newton
1984. Neymar
1985. Nic
1986. Nicholas
1987. Nick
1988. Nickolas
1989. Nicky
1990. Nico
1991. Nicolas
1992. Niel
1993. Nigel
1994. Niles
1995. Nimbus
1996. Nimrod
1997. Niko
1998. Nikolai
1999. Nikolas
2000. Niven
2001. Nixon
2002. Noah
2003. Noble
2004. Noe
2005. Noel
2006. Nolan
2007. Noland
2008. Noll
2009. Norm
2010. Norman
2011. Normand
2012. Norrie
2013. Norris
2014. Norton
2015. Norwood
2016. Nowell

O

2017. Oakley
2018. Obadiah

2019. Obed
2020. Oberon
2021. Ocean
2022. Oded
2023. Odell
2024. Odin
2025. Odran
2026. Ofer
2027. Ofir
2028. Oli
2029. Oliver
2030. Ollie
2031. Omar
2032. Omari
2033. Omega
2034. Omri
2035. Onam
2036. Oran
2037. Orian
2038. Orion
2039. Orlando
2040. Ormond
2041. Ormonde
2042. Orrell
2043. Orrin
2044. Orson
2045. Orval
2046. Orville
2047. Osbert
2048. Osborn
2049. Osbourne
2050. Oscar
2051. Osgood
2052. Osman
2053. Osmond
2054. Osvaldo
2055. Oswald
2056. Othello
2057. Othniel
2058. Otis
2059. Otniel
2060. Ottis
2061. Otto
2062. Owen
2063. Oz
2064. Ozzie
2065. Ozzy

P

2066. Pablo
2067. Pace
2068. Pacey
2069. Paddy
2070. Paden
2071. Page
2072. Paise
2073. Paisley
2074. Pallu
2075. Palmer
2076. Paris
2077. Parker
2078. Parris
2079. Parry
2080. Pat
2081. Patrick
2082. Paul
2083. Paulie
2084. Paxton

2085. Payton
2086. Pearce
2087. Pedro
2088. Peers
2089. Perce
2090. Percival
2091. Percy
2092. Peregrine
2093. Perry
2094. Pete
2095. Peter
2096. Peterkin
2097. Peyton
2098. Phelan
2099. Phelim
2100. Phil
2101. Philander
2102. Philip
2103. Philipe
2104. Phillip
2105. Phineas
2106. Phinehas
2107. Phoenix
2108. Pierce
2109. Pierre
2110. Piers
2111. Pip
2112. Piper
2113. Pippin
2114. Pompey
2115. Porter
2116. Preston
2117. Price
2118. Prince
2119. Princeton

Q

2120. Quentin
2121. Quin
2122. Quincey
2123. Quincy
2124. Quinlan
2125. Quinn
2126. Quintin
2127. Quinton

R

2128. Radcliff
2129. Radclyffe
2130. Radley
2131. Rae
2132. Rafael
2133. Rafe
2134. Raiden
2135. Rain
2136. Rainard
2137. Raleigh
2138. Ralph
2139. Ralphie
2140. Rama
2141. Ramiro
2142. Ramon
2143. Ranald
2144. Randal
2145. Randall
2146. Randell
2147. Randolf

2148. Randolph
2149. Randulf
2150. Randy
2151. Raphael
2152. Rashad
2153. Rashaun
2154. Rashawn
2155. Rastus
2156. Raul
2157. Raven
2158. Ray
2159. Rayan
2160. Rayden
2161. Raylan
2162. Raymond
2163. Raymund
2164. Raynard
2165. Rayner
2166. Read
2167. Reagan
2168. Red
2169. Redd
2170. Redmond
2171. Redmund
2172. Reece
2173. Reed
2174. Rees
2175. Reese
2176. Reg
2177. Reggie
2178. Reginald
2179. Reginold
2180. Reid
2181. Reilly
2182. Remington
2183. Remy
2184. Rene
2185. Reuben
2186. Reubhen
2187. Rex
2188. Rey
2189. Reyansh
2190. Reynard
2191. Rhett
2192. Rhys
2193. Ricardo
2194. Rich
2195. Richard
2196. Richie
2197. Rick
2198. Rickey
2199. Ricki
2200. Rickie
2201. Ricky
2202. Ridley
2203. Riel
2204. Rigby
2205. Rik
2206. Rikki
2207. Riley
2208. Rimmon
2209. Rimon
2210. Rio
2211. Riordan
2212. Ripley
2213. Ritchie
2214. River
2215. Rob
2216. Robbie
2217. Robby

2218. Robert
2219. Roberto
2220. Robin
2221. Rocco
2222. Rocky
2223. Roddy
2224. Roderic
2225. Roderick
2226. Rodge
2227. Rodger
2228. Rodney
2229. Rodolfo
2230. Rodrigo
2231. Rogelio
2232. Roger
2233. Rohan
2234. Roland
2235. Rolando
2236. Rolf
2237. Rolland
2238. Rollo
2239. Rolly
2240. Rolo
2241. Roly
2242. Roman
2243. Romeo
2244. Ron
2245. Ronald
2246. Ronan
2247. Ronin
2248. Ronnie
2249. Ronny
2250. Rorie
2251. Rory
2252. Roscoe
2253. Ross
2254. Rowan
2255. Rowen
2256. Rowland
2257. Rowley
2258. Roy
2259. Royal
2260. Royce
2261. Royle
2262. Royston
2263. Rube
2264. Ruben
2265. Rudy
2266. Rudyard
2267. Russ
2268. Russel
2269. Russell
2270. Rusty
2271. Ryan
2272. Ryder
2273. Ryker
2274. Rylan
2275. Ryland
2276. Rylee
2277. Rylen
2278. Ryley

S

2279. Sage
2280. Saladin
2281. Salah
2282. Salal
2283. Salmon

2284. Salvador
2285. Salvatore
2286. Sam
2287. Samir
2288. Sammie
2289. Sammy
2290. Samson
2291. Samuel
2292. Sander
2293. Sandford
2294. Sandy
2295. Sanford
2296. Santana
2297. Santiago
2298. Santino
2299. Santos
2300. Saul
2301. Sawyer
2302. Saxon
2303. Scot
2304. Scott
2305. Scottie
2306. Scotty
2307. Seamour
2308. Seamus
2309. Sean
2310. Sebastian
2311. Sefton
2312. Seir
2313. Sela
2314. Selah
2315. Selby
2316. Semaj
2317. Sergio
2318. Seth
2319. Seward
2320. Seymour
2321. Shad
2322. Shallum
2323. Shamer
2324. Shamir
2325. Shamus
2326. Shane
2327. Shannen
2328. Shannon
2329. Shaquille
2330. Shaul
2331. Shaun
2332. Shaw
2333. Shawn
2334. Shay
2335. Shaye
2336. Shayne
2337. Shea
2338. Sheamus
2339. Shelah
2340. Shelby
2341. Sheldon
2342. Shell
2343. Shelley
2344. Shelomi
2345. Shelton
2346. Sheridan
2347. Sherlock
2348. Sherman
2349. Sherwood
2350. Shiloh
2351. Shimea
2352. Shimei
2353. Shimhi

2354. Shimi
2355. Shylock
2356. Sib
2357. Sibald
2358. Sibbe
2359. Sid
2360. Sidney
2361. Silas
2362. Silvester
2363. Sim
2364. Simeon
2365. Simon
2366. Sincere
2367. Sinclair
2368. Siward
2369. Skuyler
2370. Sky
2371. Skylar
2372. Skyler
2373. Slade
2374. Sloan
2375. Sloane
2376. Sly
2377. Sol
2378. Solly
2379. Solomon
2380. Sonnie
2381. Sonny
2382. Soren
2383. Sorrel
2384. Sparrow
2385. Spencer
2386. Spike
2387. Spirit
2388. Stacey
2389. Stacy
2390. Stafford
2391. Stan
2392. Standish
2393. Stanford
2394. Stanley
2395. Stef
2396. Stefan
2397. Steph
2398. Stephen
2399. Sterling
2400. Stetson
2401. Steve
2402. Steven
2403. Stevie
2404. Stew
2405. Stewart
2406. Stirling
2407. Storm
2408. Stu
2409. Stuart
2410. Sullivan
2411. Sunny
2412. Sweeney
2413. Swithin
2414. Swithun
2415. Sybald
2416. Syd
2417. Sylas
2418. Sylvester

T

2419. Tad

2420. Taegan
2421. Taffy
2422. Tahath
2423. Talbot
2424. Talmai
2425. Talon
2426. Tanner
2427. Taskill
2428. Tate
2429. Tatum
2430. Tayler
2431. Taylor
2432. Teagan
2433. Teague
2434. Ted
2435. Teddy
2436. Teige
2437. Teigue
2438. Tel
2439. Teman
2440. Temani
2441. Temple
2442. Tenney
2443. Tennyson
2444. Terah
2445. Terance
2446. Terence
2447. Terrance
2448. Terrell
2449. Terrence
2450. Terry
2451. Tex
2452. Thad
2453. Thaddeus
2454. Thadeus
2455. Thady
2456. Thane
2457. Thatcher
2458. Theo
2459. Theobald
2460. Theodore
2461. Thiago
2462. Thom
2463. Thomas
2464. Thorley
2465. Thornton
2466. Thurston
2467. Tiarnan
2468. Tiberius
2469. Tibby
2470. Tiernan
2471. Tierney
2472. Tikva
2473. Tikvah
2474. Tim
2475. Timmy
2476. Timo
2477. Timothy
2478. Tiras
2479. Titan
2480. Titus
2481. Toal
2482. Tobiah
2483. Tobias
2484. Tobin
2485. Toby
2486. Tod
2487. Todd
2488. Tolbert
2489. Tolly

2490. Tom
2491. Tomas
2492. Tommi
2493. Tommie
2494. Tommy
2495. Tone
2496. Toney
2497. Tony
2498. Topher
2499. Trace
2500. Tracey
2501. Tracy
2502. Trafford
2503. Traherne
2504. Tranter
2505. Travers
2506. Travis
2507. Trent
2508. Trenton
2509. Trev
2510. Trevelyan
2511. Trevor
2512. Trey
2513. Tripp
2514. Tristan
2515. Tristen
2516. Tristin
2517. Tristian
2518. Triston
2519. Troy
2520. Trueman
2521. Truman
2522. Tubal
2523. Tucker
2524. Tucson
2525. Tudor
2526. Turlough
2527. Turner
2528. Ty
2529. Tybalt
2530. Tye
2531. Tylar
2532. Tyler
2533. Tylor
2534. Tyree
2535. Tyron
2536. Tyrone
2537. Tyrrell
2538. Tyson

U

2539. Uel
2540. Ulick
2541. Ulises
2542. Ulric
2543. Ulrick
2544. Ultan
2545. Uni
2546. Unni
2547. Upton
2548. Ur
2549. Urban
2550. Uri
2551. Uria
2552. Uriah
2553. Urian
2554. Uriel
2555. Urijah

2556. Utai
2557. Uthai
2558. Uz
2559. Uzal
2560. Uziel
2561. Uzzia
2562. Uzziah
2563. Uzziel

V

2564. Val
2565. Valentin
2566. Valentine
2567. Valentino
2568. Van
2569. Vance
2570. Vaughn
2571. Vere
2572. Vergil
2573. Vern
2574. Verne
2575. Vernon
2576. Vester
2577. Vic
2578. Vicente
2579. Vick
2580. Victor
2581. Vihaan
2582. Vin
2583. Vince
2584. Vincent
2585. Vincenzo
2586. Virgil
2587. Vortigen
2588. Vivaan

W

2589. Wade
2590. Walker
2591. Wallace
2592. Wallis
2593. Wally
2594. Walt
2595. Walter
2596. Walton
2597. Ward
2598. Warner
2599. Warren
2600. Warwick
2601. Washington
2602. Wat
2603. Watkin
2604. Wayland
2605. Waylon
2606. Wayne
2607. Weaver
2608. Webster
2609. Weldon
2610. Wendel
2611. Wesley
2612. Westley
2613. Westin
2614. Weston
2615. Whitaker
2616. Whitney
2617. Wil

2618. Wilber
2619. Wilbur
2620. Wilburn
2621. Wiley
2622. Wilf
2623. Wilford
2624. Wilfred
2625. Wilfrid
2626. Will
2627. Willard
2628. William
2629. Willie
2630. Willis
2631. Willoughby
2632. Willy
2633. Wilmer
2634. Wilmot
2635. Wilson
2636. Wilton
2637. Win
2638. Windsor
2639. Winfred
2640. Winfrid
2641. Winslow
2642. Winston
2643. Winthrop
2644. Wisdom
2645. Wolf
2646. Wolfe
2647. Wolfgang
2648. Woodrow
2649. Woody
2650. Wright
2651. Wyatt
2652. Wymond
2653. Wymund
2654. Wynn
2655. Wynne
2656. Wyot
2657. Wystan

X

2658. Xan
2659. Xander
2660. Xavier
2661. Xzavier

Y

2662. Yael
2663. Yahir
2664. Yehuda
2665. Yancey
2666. Yancy
2667. Yarwood
2668. York
2669. Ywain
2670. Yorath
2671. Yosef
2672. Yousef
2673. Yusuf

Z

2674. Zabdi
2675. Zaccai

2676. Zachariah
2677. Zach
2678. Zachary
2679. Zachery
2680. Zack
2681. Zackary
2682. Zackery
2683. Zadok
2684. Zaid
2685. Zaiden
2686. Zain
2687. Zaire
2688. Zak
2689. Zalmon
2690. Zander
2691. Zane
2692. Zavier
2693. Zayden
2694. Zayn
2695. Zayne
2696. Zebadiah
2697. Zebedee
2698. Zebina
2699. Zebinah
2700. Zebulon
2701. Zebulun
2702. Zechariah
2703. Zed
2704. Zedekiah
2705. Zefania
2706. Zeke
2707. Zeph
2708. Zephania
2709. Zephaniah
2710. Zerah
2711. Zia
2712. Zibeon
2713. Zimri
2714. Zion
2715. Zophia
2716. Zubin
2717. Zuph

Chapter 10: Index of Over 2000 Girls' Names

A

1. Aaliyah
2. Aanya
3. Aaren
4. Abaegayle
5. Abagael
6. Abbigail
7. Abbey
8. Abbi
9. Abby
10. Abi
11. Abia
12. Abigail
13. Abihail
14. Abijah
15. Abilene
16. Abra
17. Abrielle
18. Abril
19. Ada
20. Adaline
21. Adallina
22. Adalyn
23. Adalynn
24. Addie
25. Addilyn
26. Addilynn
27. Addison
28. Addisyn
29. Addy
30. Addyson
31. Adelaide
32. Adele
33. Adelina
34. Adeline
35. Adelle
36. Adelyn
37. Adelynn
38. Adena
39. Adene
40. Adi
41. Adison
42. Adisson
43. Adrea
44. Adreana
45. Adriana
46. Adrianna
47. Adrianne
48. Adrienne
49. Aeron
50. Aeryn
51. Affrica
52. Affton
53. Africa
54. Agatha
55. Aggie
56. Agnes

57. Agnus
58. Aiah
59. Aideen
60. Aila
61. Aileen
62. Ailsa
63. Aimee
64. Aimey
65. Aimie
66. Ainsley
67. Airla
68. Aisha
69. Aiyana
70. Alaina
71. Alana
72. Alani
73. Alanis
74. Alanna
75. Alannah
76. Alaya
77. Alayah
78. Alayna
79. Alaysia
80. Alberta
81. Albina
82. Alea
83. Aleah
84. Alease
85. Aleen
86. Aleena
87. Aleesha
88. Alejandra
89. Alena
90. Alene
91. Alesha
92. Alessandra
93. Alex
94. Alexa
95. Alexandra
96. Alexandrea
97. Alexandria
98. Alexia
99. Alexis
100. Alfreda
101. Alia
102. Aliana
103. Alice
104. Alicia
105. Alina
106. Aline
107. Alis
108. Alisa
109. Alisha
110. Alison
111. Alissa
112. Alisson
113. Alivia
114. Alix
115. Aliya
116. Aliyah
117. Aliza
118. Allana
119. Allanah
120. Alleen
121. Allene
122. Allie
123. Alline
124. Allison
125. Allissa
126. Ally

127. Allycia
128. Allyson
129. Alma
130. Almira
131. Alondra
132. Altair
133. Alva
134. Alyce
135. Alycia
136. Alys
137. Alysa
138. Alyse
139. Alysha
140. Alysia
141. Alyson
142. Alyssa
143. Alyssia
144. Alyvia
145. Alyx
146. Amabel
147. Amalea
148. Amalee
149. Amalia
150. Amaliya
151. Amanda
152. Amani
153. Amara
154. Amari
155. Amaryllis
156. Amaya
157. Amber
158. Amelia
159. Amelie
160. America
161. Amethyst
162. Amey
163. Ami
164. Amia
165. Amice
166. Amie
167. Amilia
168. Amity
169. Amina
170. Amira
171. Amirah
172. Amiya
173. Amiyah
174. Amy
175. Amya
176. Ana
177. Anabel
178. Anabella
179. Anabelle
180. Anahi
181. Anastacia
182. Anastasia
183. Anaya
184. Andee
185. Andi
186. Andra
187. Andrea
188. Andriana
189. Andrina
190. Andy
191. Aneta
192. Anetta
193. Anette
194. Angel
195. Angela
196. Angelica

197. Angelina
198. Angeline
199. Angelique
200. Angelle
201. Angellina
202. Angie
203. Anika
204. Anima
205. Anita
206. Anitra
207. Aniya
208. Aniyah
209. Ann
210. Anna
211. Annabel
212. Annabell
213. Annabella
214. Annabelle
215. Annabeth
216. Annalee
217. Annamae
218. Annamaria
219. Annalise
220. Anne
221. Annelisa
222. Annemae
223. Anne-Marie
224. Annetta
225. Annette
226. Annice
227. Annie
228. Annika
229. Anniston
230. Annmarie
231. Annora
232. Anona
233. Anonna
234. Anora
235. Ansley
236. Antoinette
237. Antonette
238. Antonia
239. Anya
240. April
241. Arabella
242. Aranza
243. Arden
244. Arely
245. Aria
246. Ariadne
247. Ariah
248. Ariana
249. Arianna
250. Ariel
251. Ariella
252. Arielle
253. Arin
254. Ariya
255. Ariyah
256. Arlene
257. Arlette
258. Arlie
259. Arline
260. Armani
261. Arya
262. Aryana
263. Aryanna
264. Ash
265. Ashlee
266. Ashleigh

267. Ashley
268. Ashlie
269. Ashlyn
270. Ashlynn
271. Ashton
272. Asia
273. Aspen
274. Aston
275. Astra
276. Astrid
277. Athena
278. Aubree
279. Aubrey
280. Aubri
281. Aubrianna
282. Aubrie
283. Aubriella
284. Aubrielle
285. Audrey
286. Audriana
287. Audrina
288. Augusta
289. Aura
290. Aurelia
291. Aurora
292. Austyn
293. Autumn
294. Ava
295. Avah
296. Avalon
297. Avalynn
298. Avelina
299. Aveline
300. Averi
301. Averie
302. Avery
303. Aviana
304. Avianna
305. Aya
306. Ayanna
307. Ayla
308. Ayleen
309. Aylin
310. Ayva
311. Azalea
312. Azaria
313. Azariah
314. Azura
315. Azure

B

---

316. Bab
317. Babette
318. Babs
319. Bailee
320. Bailey
321. Bambi
322. Barb
323. Barbara
324. Barbie
325. Barbra
326. Baylee
327. Bea
328. Beatrice
329. Beatrix
330. Becca
331. Becci

332. Becka
333. Becky
334. Bee
335. Bekki
336. Belen
337. Belinda
338. Bell
339. Bella
340. Belle
341. Bellinda
342. Belphoebe
343. Belynda
344. Berenice
345. Berlin
346. Bernadette
347. Bernadine
348. Bernice
349. Berniece
350. Berry
351. Berta
352. Bertha
353. Bertie
354. Beryl
355. Bess
356. Bessie
357. Bessy
358. Beth
359. Bethanie
360. Bethany
361. Bethel
362. Bethney
363. Betsy
364. Bette
365. Bettie
366. Bettina
367. Betty
368. Beverly
369. Bianca
370. Bijou
371. Billie
372. Bindy
373. Blair
374. Blanch
375. Blake
376. Blakely
377. Blondie
378. Blossom
379. Blythe
380. Bobbi
381. Bobbie
382. Bonita
383. Bonnie
384. Bonny
385. Brady
386. Braelyn
387. Braelynn
388. Braidy
389. Brandie
390. Brandy
391. Braylee
392. Breana
393. Breann
394. Breanna
395. Bree
396. Brenda
397. Brenna
398. Brett
399. Bria
400. Briana
401. Brianna

402. Briar
403. Bridget
404. Bridgette
405. Briella
406. Brielle
407. Briley
408. Brinley
409. Bristol
410. Britney
411. Britt
412. Britta
413. Brittani
414. Brittania
415. Brittany
416. Brittney
417. Bronte
418. Brook
419. Brooke
420. Brooklyn
421. Brooklynn
422. Bryana
423. Bryanna
424. Bryanne
425. Brylee
426. Bryleigh
427. Bryn
428. Brynlee
429. Brynn
430. Buffy
431. Burgundy

C

---

432. Cadence
433. Caetlin
434. Caitlin
435. Caitlyn
436. Caleigh
437. Cali
438. Callie
439. Cambria
440. Camellia
441. Cameron
442. Camila
443. Camilla
444. Camille
445. Cammie
446. Camryn
447. Candace
448. Candi
449. Candice
450. Candis
451. Candyce
452. Cara
453. Careen
454. Caren
455. Carey
456. Cari
457. Carin
458. Carina
459. Carine
460. Caris
461. Carissa
462. Carla
463. Carlee
464. Carlene
465. Carley
466. Carlie
467. Carlin

468. Carlisa
469. Carlota
470. Carly
471. Carlyn
472. Carmel
473. Carmen
474. Carol
475. Carolina
476. Caroline
477. Carolyn
478. Caron
479. Carreen
480. Carrie
481. Carry
482. Carter
483. Cary
484. Caryl
485. Caryn
486. Casey
487. Cass
488. Cassandra
489. Cassia
490. Cassidy
491. Cassie
492. Cataleya
493. Catalina
494. Cate
495. Cateline
496. Cath
497. Catharine
498. Catherine
499. Cathleen
500. Cathryn
501. Cathy
502. Catrina
503. Caylee
504. Cayley
505. Caylin
506. Cecelia
507. Cecilia
508. Cecily
509. Cedar
510. Celandine
511. Celeste
512. Celestine
513. Celia
514. Celine
515. Celinda
516. Chana
517. Chance
518. Chanel
519. Chanelle
520. Chantale
521. Chantel
522. Chantelle
523. Charissa
524. Charity
525. Charla
526. Charlee
527. Charleen
528. Charleigh
529. Charlene
530. Charley
531. Charli
532. Charlie
533. Charlotte
534. Chaya
535. Chelsea
536. Chelsey
537. Chelsie

538. Cher
539. Cherice
540. Cherie
541. Cherish
542. Cherilyn
543. Cherise
544. Cherry
545. Cheryl
546. Chevonne
547. Cheyenne
548. China
549. Chloe
550. Chris
551. Chrissie
552. Chrissy
553. Christa
554. Christabel
555. Christabelle
556. Christal
557. Christel
558. Christelle
559. Christen
560. Christi
561. Christiana
562. Christianne
563. Christie
564. Christina
565. Christine
566. Christobel
567. Christy
568. Chryssa
569. Chrystal
570. Chyna
571. Ciara
572. Cicely
573. Ciera
574. Cierra
575. Cindy
576. Ciss
577. Cissy
578. Claire
579. Clara
580. Clarabelle
581. Clare
582. Claribel
583. Clarice
584. Clarissa
585. Claudette
586. Claudia
587. Clemency
588. Clementine
589. Cleo
590. Clover
591. Coco
592. Codie
593. Cody
594. Coleen
595. Colene
596. Colette
597. Coline
598. Colleen
599. Collins
600. Collyn
601. Columbine
602. Connie
603. Constance
604. Cora
605. Coral
606. Coraline
607. Cordelia

608. Corinne
609. Cornelia
610. Corrine
611. Cortney
612. Courtney
613. Cristal
614. Cristen
615. Cristina
616. Crystal
617. Cyan
618. Cybill
619. Cyndi
620. Cynthia

D

621. Dacey
622. Dahlia
623. Daisy
624. Dakota
625. Dale
626. Daleyza
627. Dalia
628. Dalilah
629. Dallas
630. Dalya
631. Damiana
632. Dana
633. Dani
634. Danica
635. Daniela
636. Daniella
637. Danielle
638. Danika
639. Danna
640. Danni
641. Daphne
642. Dara
643. Darby
644. Darcey
645. Darcie
646. Darcy
647. Darla
648. Darleen
649. Darlene
650. Darnell
651. Darryl
652. Daryl
653. Davida
654. Dawn
655. Day
656. Dayna
657. Dayana
658. Deana
659. Deanna
660. Deanne
661. Deb
662. Debbi
663. Debbie
664. Debby
665. Debi
666. Deborah
667. Debra
668. Debs
669. Dee
670. Deena
671. Deirdre
672. Del
673. Delaney

674. Delia
675. Delila
676. Delilah
677. Della
678. Delora
679. Delores
680. Deloris
681. Delphia
682. Delphine
683. Demi
684. Deni
685. Denice
686. Deniece
687. Denisa
688. Denise
689. Derby
690. Derryl
691. Desdemona
692. Desiree
693. Destiny
694. Devan
695. Deven
696. Devon
697. Deziree
698. Di
699. Diamond
700. Diana
701. Diane
702. Diann
703. Dianna
704. Dianne
705. Didi
706. Dina
707. Dinah
708. Dixie
709. Dodi
710. Dodie
711. Dollie
712. Dolly
713. Dominica
714. Dominique
715. Donna
716. Dora
717. Dorean
718. Doreen
719. Doris
720. Dorothy
721. Dorthy
722. Dory
723. Dot
724. Dottie
725. Drew
726. Dulce
727. Dyan
728. Dylan

E

---

729. Ebony
730. Echo
731. Eda
732. Edain
733. Edda
734. Eden
735. Edie
736. Edith
737. Edithe
738. Edna
739. Ednah

740. Edweena
741. Edwena
742. Edwina
743. Edwyna
744. Edyth
745. Effi
746. Effie
747. Eileen
748. Elaina
749. Elaine
750. Elanor
751. Elayne
752. Elba
753. Eleanor
754. Elena
755. Elenora
756. Eliana
757. Elianna
758. Elin
759. Elinor
760. Elisa
761. Elisabeth
762. Elise
763. Eliza
764. Elizabeth
765. Ella
766. Elle
767. Ellen
768. Ellenor
769. Ellery
770. Elliana
771. Ellie
772. Elliot
773. Elliott
774. Ellison
775. Elly
776. Elmira
777. Eloise
778. Elouise
779. Elsa
780. Elsie
781. Elva
782. Elyse
783. Elyse
784. Elyzabeth
785. Em
786. Ember
787. Emelia
788. Emely
789. Emerald
790. Emerie
791. Emerson
792. Emersyn
793. Emery
794. Emilee
795. Emilia
796. Emilie
797. Emiline
798. Emily
799. Emma
800. Emmalee
801. Emmaline
802. Emmalyn
803. Emmalynn
804. Emmeline
805. Emmy
806. Emory
807. Emylynn
808. Enola
809. Enya

810. Eowyn
811. Epiphany
812. Epona
813. Erica
814. Erika
815. Erin
816. Erma
817. Ernestine
818. Eryn
819. Esme
820. Esmeralda
821. Essie
822. Esta
823. Estella
824. Estelle
825. Esther
826. Estrella
827. Ethel
828. Ethna
829. Etna
830. Ettie
831. Eugenia
832. Eunice
833. Eva
834. Evalyn
835. Evangeline
836. Eve
837. Evelyn
838. Evelynn
839. Everette
840. Everleigh
841. Everly
842. Evette
843. Evie
844. Evonne

F

---

845. Fae
846. Faith
847. Fanni
848. Fanny
849. Farrah
850. Farley
851. Farrah
852. Fatima
853. Fauna
854. Fawn
855. Fawna
856. Fay
857. Faye
858. Felice
859. Felicia
860. Felicity
861. Felina
862. Felisha
863. Fern
864. Fernanda
865. Finley
866. Finola
867. Fiona
868. Flo
869. Flora
870. Flore
871. Florence
872. Flori
873. Fran
874. Frances
875. Francesca
876. Frankie

877. Frannie
878. Frea
879. Freda
880. Fredda
881. Freddie
882. Frederica
883. Freida
884. Freya
885. Frida

G

886. Gabbie
887. Gabi
888. Gabriela
889. Gabriella
890. Gabrielle
891. Gaby
892. Gail
893. Gale
894. Galilea
895. Gardenia
896. Garnette
897. Gayle
898. Geena
899. Gemma
900. Gena
901. Genesis
902. Geneva
903. Genevieve
904. Georgeanna
905. Georgene
906. Georgette
907. Georgia
908. Georgiana
909. Georgie
910. Georgina
911. Georgine
912. Geraldine
913. Gerry
914. Gertie
915. Gertrude
916. Gia
917. Giana
918. Gianna
919. Gillian
920. Gina
921. Ginger
922. Ginnie
923. Ginny
924. Giovanna
925. Giselle
926. Giuliana
927. Gladys
928. Glenda
929. Glenice
930. Glenys
931. Gloria
932. Grace
933. Gracelyn
934. Gracelynn
935. Gracie
936. Greta
937. Gretchen
938. Gretel
939. Gretta
940. Guadalupe
941. Guendolen
942. Gwen

943. Gwendolyn
944. Gweneth
945. Gwenn
946. Gwenneth
947. Gwennyth
948. Gwyn
949. Gytha

H

950. Hadassah
951. Hadlee
952. Hadleigh
953. Hadley
954. Haidee
955. Hailee
956. Hailey
957. Haley
958. Halle
959. Hallie
960. Hana
961. Hanna
962. Hannah
963. Hannie
964. Harlee
965. Harley
966. Harlow
967. Harmony
968. Harper
969. Harriet
970. Harriett
971. Harrietta
972. Harriette
973. Hattie
974. Hatty
975. Haven
976. Haydee
977. Hayden
978. Haylee
979. Hayleigh
980. Hayley
981. Hazel
982. Heather
983. Heaven
984. Hebe
985. Heidi
986. Helaine
987. Heleen
988. Helen
989. Helena
990. Helene
991. Helga
992. Hellen
993. Henley
994. Henrietta
995. Hester
996. Hilary
997. Hilda
998. Hillary
999. Holland
1000. Hollie
1001. Hollis
1002. Holly
1003. Honey
1004. Honor
1005. Honour
1006. Hope
1007. Hortense
1008. Hosanna

1009. Hosannah
1010. Hunter
1011. Hylda

I

1012. Ida
1013. Idelle
1014. Iesha
1015. Ilene
1016. Iliana
1017. Imani
1018. Imogen
1019. Imogene
1020. Ina
1021. India
1022. Indiana
1023. Indigo
1024. Indy
1025. Ingrid
1026. Ireland
1027. Irene
1028. Iris
1029. Irma
1030. Isabel
1031. Isabela
1032. Isabella
1033. Isabelle
1034. Isadora
1035. Isis
1036. Isla
1037. Isolde
1038. Itzel
1039. Ivanna
1040. Ivory
1041. Ivy
1042. Izabella
1043. Izzy

J

1044. Jacinda
1045. Jackaline
1046. Jackalyn
1047. Jacki
1048. Jackie
1049. Jacklyn
1050. Jacqueline
1051. Jada
1052. Jade
1053. Jaden
1054. Jadyn
1055. Jaelyn
1056. Jaelynn
1057. Jaida
1058. Jaime
1059. Jaimee
1060. Jaki
1061. Jakki
1062. Jaliyah
1063. Jamie
1064. Janae
1065. Jane
1066. Janel
1067. Janella
1068. Janelle
1069. Janene
1070. Janessa

1071. Janet
1072. Janetta
1073. Janette
1074. Janey
1075. Janice
1076. Janie
1077. Janine
1078. Janis
1079. Janiya
1080. Janiyah
1081. Janna
1082. Jannah
1083. Jannette
1084. Jannine
1085. Jaqueline
1086. Jaquelyn
1087. Jasmin
1088. Jasmine
1089. Jasmyn
1090. Jaycee
1091. Jayda
1092. Jayde
1093. Jayden
1094. Jayla
1095. Jaylah
1096. Jaylee
1097. Jayleen
1098. Jaylene
1099. Jaylin
1100. Jaylynn
1101. Jayme
1102. Jayne
1103. Jaynie
1104. Jazlyn
1105. Jazlynn
1106. Jazmin
1107. Jazmine
1108. Jean
1109. Jeana
1110. Jeanette
1111. Jeanie
1112. Jeanine
1113. Jeanna
1114. Jeannette
1115. Jeannie
1116. Jeannine
1117. Jedidah
1118. Jemma
1119. Jen
1120. Jenna
1121. Jenelle
1122. Jenessa
1123. Jennifer
1124. Jenny
1125. Jerri
1126. Jerrie
1127. Jerry
1128. Jess
1129. Jessa
1130. Jessalyn
1131. Jessica
1132. Jessie
1133. Jetta
1134. Jewel
1135. Jezebel
1136. Jill
1137. Jillian
1138. Jillie
1139. Jilly
1140. Jimena

1141. Jinny
1142. Jo
1143. Joan
1144. Joanna
1145. Joanne
1146. Joceline
1147. Jocelyn
1148. Jocelynn
1149. Jodi
1150. Jodie
1151. Jody
1152. Joelle
1153. Johanna
1154. Joi
1155. Jojo
1156. Joleen
1157. Jolene
1158. Jolie
1159. Jonette
1160. Joni
1161. Jordan
1162. Jordana
1163. Jordie
1164. Jordon
1165. Jordyn
1166. Jordynn
1167. Joselyn
1168. Josephine
1169. Josette
1170. Josie
1171. Joslyn
1172. Joss
1173. Josslyn
1174. Journee
1175. Journey
1176. Joy
1177. Joyce
1178. Judith
1179. Judy
1180. Jules
1181. Julia
1182. Juliana
1183. Julianna
1184. Julianne
1185. Julie
1186. Juliet
1187. Julieta
1188. Juliette
1189. Julissa
1190. July
1191. June
1192. Juniper
1193. Justice

K

1194. Kacey
1195. Kacie
1196. Kadence
1197. Kae
1198. Kaelea
1199. Kaelee
1200. Kaelyn
1201. Kaelynn
1202. Kai
1203. Kaia
1204. Kaidence
1205. Kailani
1206. Kailee

1207. Kailey
1208. Kailyn
1209. Kairi
1210. Kaitlyn
1211. Kaitlynn
1212. Kaiya
1213. Kaleigh
1214. Kaley
1215. Kali
1216. Kalie
1217. Kalisha
1218. Kaliyah
1219. Kalla
1220. Kallie
1221. Kalyn
1222. Kalysta
1223. Kamila
1224. Kamryn
1225. Kandace
1226. Kandi
1227. Kara
1228. Karen
1229. Karena
1230. Karenza
1231. Kari
1232. Karina
1233. Karissa
1234. Karla
1235. Karlee
1236. Karlene
1237. Karlie
1238. Karly
1239. Karolyn
1240. Karon
1241. Karrie
1242. Karsyn
1243. Karter
1244. Karyna
1245. Kasey
1246. Kassandra
1247. Kassia
1248. Kassidy
1249. Kassy
1250. Kat
1251. Katalina
1252. Kate
1253. Katelin
1254. Katelyn
1255. Katelynn
1256. Katey
1257. Kath
1258. Katharine
1259. Katharyn
1260. Katharyne
1261. Katherin
1262. Katherine
1263. Kathleen
1264. Kathlyn
1265. Kathryn
1266. Kathy
1267. Katie
1268. Katlyn
1269. Katrina
1270. Katryna
1271. Katy
1272. Kay
1273. Kaycee
1274. Kayden
1275. Kaydence
1276. Kayla

1277. Kayleah
1278. Kaylee
1279. Kayleen
1280. Kayleigh
1281. Kayley
1282. Kaylie
1283. Kaylin
1284. Kayly
1285. Kaylynn
1286. Keara
1287. Keelan
1288. Keira
1289. Keisha
1290. Keitha
1291. Kelcey
1292. Kelia
1293. Kell
1294. Kelleigh
1295. Kelly
1296. Kelsey
1297. Kenda
1298. Kendal
1299. Kendall
1300. Kendra
1301. Kenia
1302. Kenina
1303. Kenley
1304. Kenna
1305. Kennedi
1306. Kennedy
1307. Kensley
1308. Kenya
1309. Kenzie
1310. Keren
1311. Kerena
1312. Keri
1313. Kerri
1314. Kerrie
1315. Kerry
1316. Kerstin
1317. Keshia
1318. Kestrel
1319. Keyla
1320. Keysha
1321. Kezia
1322. Keziah
1323. Khaleesi
1324. Khloe
1325. Kiana
1326. Kiara
1327. Kiera
1328. Kiersten
1329. Kiley
1330. Kiki
1331. Kiley
1332. Kim
1333. Kimber
1334. Kimberlee
1335. Kimberleigh
1336. Kimberley
1337. Kimberly
1338. Kimberlyn
1339. Kimbra
1340. Kimmy
1341. Kimora
1342. Kingsley
1343. Kinley
1344. Kinslee
1345. Kinsley
1346. Kira

1347. Kirsteen
1348. Kirsten
1349. Kora
1350. Kori
1351. Kristen
1352. Kirstie
1353. Kirstin
1354. Kit
1355. Kristina
1356. Kody
1357. Kourtney
1358. Kris
1359. Krissy
1360. Krista
1361. Kristal
1362. Kristeen
1363. Kristin
1364. Kristina
1365. Kristine
1366. Kristy
1367. Krysten
1368. Kyla
1369. Kylah
1370. Kylee
1371. Kyleigh
1372. Kylie
1373. Kym
1374. Kynlee
1375. Kyra

L

1376. Lacey
1377. Lacie
1378. Lacy
1379. Laila
1380. Lailah
1381. Lainey
1382. Lana
1383. Landry
1384. Laney
1385. Lara
1386. Laraine
1387. Lark
1388. Lashawn
1389. Lashonda
1390. Latisha
1391. Latoya
1392. Laura
1393. Lauraine
1394. Laureen
1395. Laurel
1396. Laurelle
1397. Lauren
1398. Laurencia
1399. Laurie
1400. Laurine
1401. Laurissa
1402. Lauryn
1403. Lavender
1404. Lavern
1405. Layla
1406. Laylah
1407. Layton
1408. Lea
1409. Leah
1410. Leann
1411. Leanna
1412. Leanora

1413. Leda
1414. Lee
1415. Leena
1416. Leia
1417. Leighton
1418. Leila
1419. Leilani
1420. Lena
1421. Lennon
1422. Lenora
1423. Lenore
1424. Leona
1425. Leone
1426. Leonora
1427. Leonore
1428. Les
1429. Lesleigh
1430. Lesley
1431. Leslie
1432. Lesly
1433. Letitia
1434. Lettie
1435. Lex
1436. Lexi
1437. Lexie
1438. Leyla
1439. Lia
1440. Liana
1441. Libbie
1442. Libby
1443. Liberty
1444. Liddy
1445. Lila
1446. Lilac
1447. Lilah
1448. Lilia
1449. Lilian
1450. Liliana
1451. Lilianna
1452. Lilith
1453. Lillian
1454. Lilliana
1455. Lillianna
1456. Lillie
1457. Lilly
1458. Lily
1459. Lilyana
1460. Lilyanna
1461. Lina
1462. Linda
1463. Lindsay
1464. Lindsey
1465. Lindsie
1466. Lindy
1467. Linette
1468. Linn
1469. Linnet
1470. Linnette
1471. Linnie
1472. Linsay
1473. Linsey
1474. Lis
1475. Lisa
1476. Lisanne
1477. Lisbeth
1478. Lisha
1479. Lissa
1480. Liv
1481. Livia
1482. Liza

1483. Lizbeth
1484. Lizzie
1485. Logan
1486. Lois
1487. Lola
1488. London
1489. Londyn
1490. Lor
1491. Lora
1492. Loraine
1493. Lorainne
1494. Lorayne
1495. Loreen
1496. Lorelai
1497. Lorelei
1498. Lori
1499. Lorie
1500. Lorin
1501. Lorina
1502. Lorraine
1503. Lorri
1504. Lottie
1505. Lou
1506. Louella
1507. Louisa
1508. Louise
1509. Lucia
1510. Luciana
1511. Lucille
1512. Lucy
1513. Luella
1514. Luna
1515. Lunet
1516. Lux
1517. Lyda
1518. Lydia
1519. Lyla
1520. Lylah
1521. Lynda
1522. Lyndi
1523. Lyndsay
1524. Lynet
1525. Lynette
1526. Lynn
1527. Lynna
1528. Lynne
1529. Lynnette
1530. Lyra
1531. Lyric
1532. Lys
1533. Lysandra
1534. Lysanne
1535. Lysette
1536. Lyssa

M

1537. Mabel
1538. Maybella
1539. Mable
1540. Macey
1541. Maci
1542. Macie
1543. Mackenzie
1544. Macy
1545. Madalyn
1546. Madalynn

1547. Maddie
1548. Maddison
1549. Madeleine
1550. Madeline
1551. Madelyn
1552. Madelynn
1553. Madge
1554. Madilyn
1555. Madilynn
1556. Madison
1557. Madisyn
1558. Madlyn
1559. Madoline
1560. Madonna
1561. Madyson
1562. Mae
1563. Maegan
1564. Maev
1565. Maeva
1566. Maeve
1567. Maeveen
1568. Mag
1569. Magdalen
1570. Magdalena
1571. Magdalene
1572. Maggie
1573. Magnolia
1574. Maia
1575. Maisie
1576. Makayla
1577. Makenna
1578. Makenzie
1579. Malaya
1580. Malaysia
1581. Maleah
1582. Malia
1583. Maliah
1584. Malinda
1585. Maliyah
1586. Mallory
1587. Malvina
1588. Mamie
1589. Mandi
1590. Mandy
1591. Mara
1592. Maralyn
1593. Marcelyn
1594. Marci
1595. Marcia
1596. Marcie
1597. Marcy
1598. Margaret
1599. Margarita
1600. Marge
1601. Margery
1602. Margie
1603. Margo
1604. Margot
1605. Maria
1606. Mariah
1607. Mariam
1608. Marian
1609. Mariana
1610. Marianna
1611. Marianne
1612. Marie
1613. Mariel
1614. Marigold
1615. Marilyn
1616. Marilynn

1617. Marina
1618. Marinda
1619. Maris
1620. Marisa
1621. Marise
1622. Marisol
1623. Marissa
1624. Mariyah
1625. Marje
1626. Marjorie
1627. Marjory
1628. Marla
1629. Marlee
1630. Marleen
1631. Marleigh
1632. Marlene
1633. Marley
1634. Marlie
1635. Marly
1636. Marlyn
1637. Marsha
1638. Marshan
1639. Marta
1640. Martha
1641. Martina
1642. Mary
1643. Maryam
1644. Maryann
1645. Maryanna
1646. Maryanne
1647. Marybeth
1648. Marylou
1649. Marylyn
1650. Mathilda
1651. Matilda
1652. Mattie
1653. Matty
1654. Maud
1655. Maude
1656. Maureen
1657. Maurene
1658. Maurine
1659. Mavis
1660. Maxene
1661. Maxine
1662. May
1663. Maya
1664. Maybelle
1665. Maybelline
1666. Mckayla
1667. Mckenna
1668. Mckenzie
1669. Mckinley
1670. Meadow
1671. Meagan
1672. Meg
1673. Megan
1674. Meggie
1675. Mel
1676. Melanie
1677. Melany
1678. Melina
1679. Melinda
1680. Melissa
1681. Mellony
1682. Melody
1683. Mercedes
1684. Mercia
1685. Mercy
1686. Meredith

1687. Meridith
1688. Merideth
1689. Meriel
1690. Merilyn
1691. Merrill
1692. Merry
1693. Meryl
1694. Mia
1695. Miah
1696. Micah
1697. Michaela
1698. Michayla
1699. Michelle
1700. Midge
1701. Mikaela
1702. Mikayla
1703. Mila
1704. Milan
1705. Milana
1706. Milani
1707. Milania
1708. Mildred
1709. Mildreth
1710. Milena
1711. Miley
1712. Milicent
1713. Milisent
1714. Millie
1715. Milly
1716. Mina
1717. Mindy
1718. Minnie
1719. Mira
1720. Mirabel
1721. Miracle
1722. Miranda
1723. Miriam
1724. Missie
1725. Missy
1726. Misti
1727. Misty
1728. Miya
1729. Mo
1730. Moira
1731. Moll
1732. Mollie
1733. Molly
1734. Mona
1735. Monica
1736. Monroe
1737. Monserrat
1738. Montana
1739. Montserrat
1740. Moreen
1741. Morgan
1742. Morgana
1743. Morgen
1744. Moriah
1745. Moyra
1746. Muriel
1747. Mya
1748. Myah
1749. Myla
1750. Myra
1751. Myranda
1752. Myriam
1753. Myrtle

N

1754. Nadia
1755. Nadine
1756. Nala
1757. Nancy
1758. Nanette
1759. Nanna
1760. Naomi
1761. Natalee
1762. Natalia
1763. Natalie
1764. Nataly
1765. Natalya
1766. Natasha
1767. Nathalie
1768. Nathaly
1769. Naya
1770. Nayeli
1771. Nell
1772. Nella
1773. Nellie
1774. Nelly
1775. Neriah
1776. Nessa
1777. Nessie
1778. Nettie
1779. Nevada
1780. Nevaeh
1781. Nia
1782. Nichole
1783. Nicky
1784. Nicola
1785. Nicole
1786. Nicolette
1787. Nikki
1788. Nikkole
1789. Nina
1790. Noa
1791. Noella
1792. Noelle
1793. Noemi
1794. Nola
1795. Nolene
1796. Nona
1797. Noni
1798. Nora
1799. Norah
1800. Noreen
1801. Norene
1802. Norma
1803. Nova
1804. Nydia
1805. Nyla
1806. Nylah

O

1807. Oakley
1808. Oanez
1809. Octavia
1810. Oda
1811. Olive
1812. Olivette
1813. Olivia
1814. Ollie
1815. Olyvia
1816. Ondrea

1817. Opal
1818. Ophelia
1819. Oprah
1820. Orchid
1821. Oriana
1822. Oriane
1823. Orianne
1824. Owena

P

1825. Page
1826. Paget
1827. Paige
1828. Paise
1829. Paislee
1830. Paisley
1831. Paityn
1832. Paloma
1833. Pam
1834. Pamela
1835. Pansy
1836. Paola
1837. Paris
1838. Parker
1839. Patience
1840. Patricia
1841. Patsy
1842. Patti
1843. Patty
1844. Paula
1845. Pauleen
1846. Paulene
1847. Paulette
1848. Paulina
1849. Pauline
1850. Payton
1851. Pearl
1852. Pearlie
1853. Peg
1854. Peggie
1855. Peggy
1856. Pen
1857. Penelope
1858. Penny
1859. Perdita
1860. Perla
1861. Petra
1862. Petunia
1863. Peyton
1864. Phebe
1865. Phoebe
1866. Phoenix
1867. Piper
1868. Pollie
1869. Polly
1870. Pollyanna
1871. Poppy
1872. Portia
1873. Posey
1874. Posie
1875. Posy
1876. Presley
1877. Primrose
1878. Pris
1879. Priscilla
1880. Prudence
1881. Prue
1882. Purdie

1883. Pyper

Q

1884. Quinn
1885. Queenie

R

1886. Rachael
1887. Racheal
1888. Rachel
1889. Racquel
1890. Rae
1891. Raegan
1892. Raelyn
1893. Raelynn
1894. Raina
1895. Randi
1896. Raphaela
1897. Raquel
1898. Raven
1899. Ravenna
1900. Raylene
1901. Raymonda
1902. Rayna
1903. Rayne
1904. Reagan
1905. Reanna
1906. Reba
1907. Rebecca
1908. Rebekah
1909. Reese
1910. Regina
1911. Reina
1912. Remi
1913. Remington
1914. Remy
1915. Renata
1916. Renee
1917. Reyna
1918. Rhianna
1919. Rhoda
1920. Ria
1921. Richelle
1922. Rika
1923. Riley
1924. Ripley
1925. Rita
1926. River
1927. Rivka
1928. Riya
1929. Robbie
1930. Roberta
1931. Robin
1932. Robynne
1933. Rona
1934. Ronda
1935. Ronnette
1936. Ronnie
1937. Rory
1938. Rosa
1939. Rosabel
1940. Rosaleen
1941. Rosalie
1942. Rosalin
1943. Rosalyn
1944. Rose

1945. Roseann
1946. Roseanne
1947. Roselyn
1948. Rosemarie
1949. Rosemary
1950. Rosie
1951. Roslyn
1952. Rosy
1953. Rowan
1954. Rowena
1955. Rowina
1956. Roxana
1957. Roxane
1958. Roxanna
1959. Roxanne
1960. Roxie
1961. Roxy
1962. Roz
1963. Rozanne
1964. Rubie
1965. Ruby
1966. Ruth
1967. Ryan
1968. Ryana
1969. Ryanne
1970. Rylan
1971. Rylee
1972. Ryleigh
1973. Rylie

S

1974. Sabina
1975. Sable
1976. Sabrina
1977. Sabryna
1978. Sadie
1979. Saffie
1980. Saffron
1981. Sage
1982. Saige
1983. Sal
1984. Salena
1985. Salina
1986. Salli
1987. Sallie
1988. Sally
1989. Salma
1990. Salome
1991. Sam
1992. Samantha
1993. Samara
1994. Samiyah
1995. Sammi
1996. Sammie
1997. Sandie
1998. Sandra
1999. Sandy
2000. Saniyah
2001. Sapphire
2002. Sara
2003. Sarah
2004. Sarahjeanne
2005. Sarai
2006. Sariah
2007. Sarina
2008. Sasha
2009. Saundra
2010. Savanna

2011. Savannah
2012. Sawyer
2013. Saylor
2014. Scarlet
2015. Scarlett
2016. Scarlette
2017. Scout
2018. Seanna
2019. Sedona
2020. Selah
2021. Selena
2022. Selina
2023. Selma
2024. Seona
2025. Serena
2026. Serenity
2027. Shae
2028. Shaelyn
2029. Shan
2030. Shana
2031. Shanelle
2032. Shanene
2033. Shania
2034. Shannon
2035. Shantae
2036. Shantel
2037. Shantelle
2038. Sharalyn
2039. Sharleen
2040. Sharlene
2041. Sharon
2042. Sharron
2043. Sharyl
2044. Sharyn
2045. Shauna
2046. Shawna
2047. Shawnda
2048. Shawndee
2049. Shay
2050. Shayla
2051. Shaylyn
2052. Shayne
2053. Shea
2054. Sheena
2055. Sheenagh
2056. Sheila
2057. Shelby
2058. Shelley
2059. Shena
2060. Sheona
2061. Sherah
2062. Sheri
2063. Sherie
2064. Sherill
2065. Sherilyn
2066. Sherlyn
2067. Sheryl
2068. Shevaun
2069. Shevon
2070. Shiloh
2071. Shirley
2072. Shyla
2073. Sibyl
2074. Sidney
2075. Siena
2076. Sienna
2077. Sierra
2078. Silvia
2079. Simone
2080. Sindy

2081. Sissie
2082. Sissy
2083. Sky
2084. Skye
2085. Skyla
2086. Skylar
2087. Skyler
2088. Sloan
2089. Sloane
2090. Sofia
2091. Sommer
2092. Sondra
2093. Sonia
2094. Sonora
2095. Sophia
2096. Sophie
2097. Sophy
2098. Sorrel
2099. Sparrow
2100. Stacee
2101. Stacey
2102. Stacy
2103. Star
2104. Starla
2105. Stef
2106. Stefanie
2107. Steffie
2108. Stella
2109. Steph
2110. Stephanie
2111. Stephany
2112. Stevie
2113. Storm
2114. Sue
2115. Suellen
2116. Sukie
2117. Summer
2118. Sunny
2119. Susan
2120. Susana
2121. Susanna
2122. Susannah
2123. Susanne
2124. Suse
2125. Susie
2126. Sutton
2127. Suzan
2128. Suzanna
2129. Suzanne
2130. Suzette
2131. Suzie
2132. Suzy
2133. Sybil
2134. Sybilla
2135. Syd
2136. Sydney
2137. Sylva
2138. Sylvia

T

2139. Tabatha
2140. Tabby
2141. Tabitha
2142. Talia
2143. Talisha
2144. Taliyah
2145. Tallula
2146. Tallulah

2147. Tami
2148. Tamia
2149. Tamika
2150. Tammara
2151. Tammie
2152. Tammy
2153. Tamsen
2154. Tamson
2155. Tamsyn
2156. Tania
2157. Tanner
2158. Tansy
2159. Tara
2160. Tarah
2161. Tarina
2162. Taryn
2163. Tatiana
2164. Tatum
2165. Taylor
2166. Tayler
2167. Teagan
2168. Tegan
2169. Temperance
2170. Tempest
2171. Temple
2172. Tenley
2173. Tera
2174. Terah
2175. Teresa
2176. Teri
2177. Terra
2178. Terri
2179. Terry
2180. Tess
2181. Tessa
2182. Tessie
2183. Thalia
2184. Thea
2185. Theda
2186. Thelma
2187. Theresa
2188. Thomasina
2189. Tia
2190. Tiana
2191. Tianna
2192. Tiara
2193. Tibby
2194. Tiffani
2195. Tiffany
2196. Tina
2197. Tiphanie
2198. Tisha
2199. Tonya
2200. Tori
2201. Toya
2202. Tracey
2203. Tracie
2204. Tracy
2205. Tria
2206. Tricia
2207. Trina
2208. Trinity
2209. Trish
2210. Trisha
2211. Trista
2212. Trix
2213. Trixie
2214. Trudi
2215. Trudy
2216. Twila

U

2217. Ula
2218. Ulrica
2219. Una
2220. Unice
2221. Ursula

V

2222. Val
2223. Valentina
2224. Valeria
2225. Valerie
2226. Valorie
2227. Vanessa
2228. Veda
2229. Vera
2230. Veronica
2231. Veronique
2232. Vi
2233. Vicki
2234. Vicky
2235. Victoria
2236. Viola
2237. Violet
2238. Virginia
2239. Vivian
2240. Viviana
2241. Vivien
2242. Vivienne

W

2243. Wanda
2244. Wenda
2245. Wendy
2246. Wenona
2247. Whitney
2248. Wilda
2249. Willa
2250. Willow
2251. Wilma
2252. Win
2253. Winifred
2254. Winona
2255. Winter
2256. Wren
2257. Wynne
2258. Wynonna
2259. Wynter

X

2260. Xara
2261. Xena
2262. Ximena

Y

2263. Yamileth
2264. Yareli

2265. Yaretzi
2266. Yaritza
2267. Yasmin
2268. Yolanda
2269. Yvette
2270. Yvonne

Z

2271. Zahra
2272. Zainab
2273. Zaniyah
2274. Zara
2275. Zaria
2276. Zariah
2277. Zariyah
2278. Zelda
2279. Zelia
2280. Zelma
2281. Zendaya
2282. Zion
2283. Zoe
2284. Zoey
2285. Zoie
2286. Zuri

Chapter 11: Obscure and Interesting Names

Are you looking for something a little more unique? According to the American Social Security Administration, these names appear with very low frequency.

Over 400 Unique Boys' Names

A

1. Aaliyah
2. Aariyan
3. Aaroh
4. Aavyan
5. Abaan
6. Abdirahim
7. Abdulmajid
8. Aben
9. Abiezer
10. Abubakarr
11. Acer
12. Adison
13. Adom
14. Adoni
15. Adrial
16. Adwaith
17. Airick
18. Airin
19. Akarsh
20. Akiles
21. Alaa
22. Alber
23. Allijah
24. Alyk
25. Alyxzander
26. Amadi
27. Amais
28. Amaurie
29. Ameya
30. Andric
31. Anil
32. Anyelo
33. Arcangelo
34. Arieh
35. Arly
36. Armonte
37. Arrion
38. Arsene
39. Ashan

40. Ashaun
41. Ashvath
42. Athanasius
43. Athens
44. Audrey
45. Aurin
46. Avedis
47. Averey
48. Avondre
49. Avraj
50. Ayres
51. Azarael
52. Azarian

B

53. Baby
54. Bangaly
55. Barett
56. Beni
57. Berat
58. Bevan
59. Billion
60. Blace
61. Blaz
62. Bohannon
63. Bonifacio
64. Bradlyn
65. Brahim
66. Brevon
67. Brextyn
68. Brilynn
69. Brittain
70. Buruk

C

71. Caetano
72. Calab
73. Calev
74. Callin
75. Calvary
76. Camarri
77. Carlon
78. Casson
79. Cayetano
80. Chanden
81. Chigozie
82. Chikamso
83. Chrystopher
84. Chukwuka
85. Claytin
86. Coalson
87. Common
88. Conlon
89. Corron
90. Cresencio
91. Crews
92. Cruse
93. Crystopher

D

94. Dacorian
95. Dakobe
96. Dalin
97. Damare
98. Damonee

99. Damonii
100. Danell
101. Danton
102. Danylo
103. Dar
104. Daran
105. Dardan
106. Davaun
107. Davionne
108. Davud
109. Daymein
110. Deakyn
111. Deason
112. Dekendrick
113. Delshawn
114. Demonei
115. Demont
116. Denham
117. Denys
118. Deryk
119. Desmen
120. Destined
121. Devone
122. Devraj
123. Deyvid
124. Dheera
125. Donal
126. Donjuan
127. Donovon
128. Dovi
129. Drae
130. Drayvin
131. Drazen
132. Drezden

E

133. Edenilson
134. Edsel
135. Edwynn
136. Efosa
137. Eker
138. Elise
139. Elisee
140. Elizander
141. Elnatan
142. Elyjiah
143. Emaan
144. Emar
145. Emeterio
146. Emiel
147. Emier
148. Erioluwa
149. Erza
150. Essey
151. Estevon
152. Evelyn
153. Evens
154. Everly
155. Ezykiel
156. Faruq
157. Fawzan
158. Feliks
159. Fender
160. Fields
161. Forrester
162. Frandy

G

163. Gamble
164. Georgie
165. Georgiy
166. Georgy
167. Gerhard
168. Giddeon
169. Girish
170. Grasen
171. Grier
172. Grigory
173. Gurshan

H

174. Haaken
175. Halil
176. Hammond
177. Hamze
178. Harut
179. Hasib
180. Hayward
181. Henon
182. Hezakiah
183. Hinson
184. Hiyab
185. Holder
186. Homar
187. Honour
188. Hriday
189. Huntlee
190. Hussien

I

191. Ikechi
192. Illyas
193. Isias
194. Itiel
195. Izach
196. Izeiah
197. Izyk
198. Izzaiah

J

199. Jacaiden
200. Jacione
201. Jacorion
202. Jadir
203. Jadore
204. Jaharie
205. Jahbari
206. Jahmil
207. Jahshua
208. Jaishawn
209. Jaivian
210. Jaizen
211. Jaizon
212. Jakylan
213. Jakyle
214. Jakyren
215. Jamespatrick
216. Jamorris
217. Jamus
218. Janard

219. Jandriel
220. Jarrius
221. Jash
222. Jasyn
223. Jatin
224. Jawaan
225. Jaxs
226. Jaxstin
227. Jaycek
228. Jayin
229. Jazer
230. Jazib
231. Jemar
232. Jerian
233. Jerman
234. Jermane
235. Jersiah
236. Jettsen
237. Jhai
238. Jhan
239. Jmichael
240. Joanna
241. Johngabriel
242. Jolen
243. Jolyon
244. Jonaven
245. Jonelle
246. Jonh
247. Jonni
248. Josaih
249. Josten
250. Jozy
251. Jrayden
252. Jud
253. Junah
254. Junhao
255. Jusuf
256. Juwon
257. Jyron

K

258. Kager
259. Kahekili
260. Kaido
261. Kaimen
262. Kaisin
263. Kamali
264. Kamare
265. Kamaree
266. Kamir
267. Karden
268. Karion
269. Karloz
270. Karrar
271. Kass
272. Kaushal
273. Keatin
274. Kelii
275. Kenil
276. Ketan
277. Keveon
278. Keyen
279. Keymonie
280. Khamir
281. Khaos
282. Kholten
283. Khristan
284. Kingdon

285. Kingstan
286. Kinson
287. Koray
288. Kostantinos
289. Kriss
290. Kruize
291. Kupono
292. Kwamane
293. Kydan
294. Kyus
295. Kyven

L

296. Laif
297. Lakyn
298. Lamareon
299. Lameir
300. Lansing
301. Leeo
302. Legendary
303. Lens
304. Levion
305. Lexandro
306. Liamalexander
307. Ludovic
308. Ludwin
309. Lynkon
310. Lynwood

M

311. Mach
312. Mackinley
313. Madoxx
314. Malechi
315. Manfred
316. Manvik
317. Marcellis
318. Marquavious
319. Marrion
320. Masahiro
321. Mascen
322. Mathais
323. Mavin
324. Maxxen
325. Mcconnell
326. Medhansh
327. Melton
328. Merlyn
329. Meshal
330. Messyah
331. Mikhale
332. Mikiah
333. Mojtaba
334. Mokshith
335. Molly
336. Monish
337. Motty
338. Mourya
339. Mozart
340. Mylin

N

341. Nabhan
342. Nabhya

343. Najae
344. Nathaneil
345. Nazire
346. Neill
347. Nekhi
348. Nhan
349. Nickolis
350. Nikolus
351. Nirek
352. Nivin
353. Nixin
354. Noman
355. Nora
356. Novel
357. Nowah

O

358. Odis
359. Oladimeji
360. Oluwakayode
361. Ovidio

P

362. Paetyn
363. Parmeet
364. Patriot
365. Phanuel
366. Phinn
367. Prabin
368. Prajit
369. Prayash

Q

370. Quandarius
371. Quantae
372. Quartez
373. Quatavious
374. Quenten
375. Quill
376. Quintel

R

377. Radford
378. Rahmeek
379. Rahmere
380. Rakye
381. Ramie
382. Ranferi
383. Ranson
384. Raoul
385. Rasool
386. Rayburn
387. Raymar
388. Remus
389. Rendon
390. Rhet
391. Rhyley
392. Rhylin
393. Rishawn
394. Riston
395. Riyon
396. Rodel
397. Roey

398. Rolf
399. Rooks
400. Rosco
401. Roshad
402. Rozay
403. Rushank
404. Ryat

S

---

405. Saba
406. Saben
407. Sabriel
408. Sadman
409. Safari
410. Samere
411. Samrudh
412. Samuele
413. Samvel
414. Sascha
415. Seiya
416. Selwyn
417. Shahaan
418. Shanard
419. Shep
420. Sheya
421. Shivaansh
422. Shreehan
423. Shylo
424. Sidahmed
425. Sirwilliam
426. Soryn
427. Spyridon
428. Stephenson
429. Stevin
430. Sudeys
431. Sybastian
432. Syheem

T

---

433. Taeson
434. Tannar
435. Tarrel
436. Tarren
437. Taygen
438. Teighan
439. Terek
440. Terrius
441. Terryn
442. Teshaun
443. Tesher
444. Theran
445. Torri
446. Torris
447. Tou
448. Traeger
449. Traivon
450. Trayshawn
451. Tredyn
452. Trendan
453. Treson
454. Trestan
455. Trishan
456. Tycere
457. Tyme
458. Tyrez
459. Tyrome

460. Tywaun

U

461. Ugonna

V

462. Valiant
463. Vardan
464. Vasily
465. Veyron
466. Vicktor
467. Victorhugo
468. Vivian

W

469. Waldemar
470. Waldo
471. Wenceslao
472. Willaim
473. Wolfram
474. Wyman

X

475. Xain
476. Xaniel
477. Xaver
478. Xzaiden

Y

479. Yancarlo
480. Yaniv
481. Yaw
482. Yazziel
483. Yexiel
484. Yiran
485. Yoscar
486. Yugo
487. Yushin

Z

488. Zaaron
489. Zacai
490. Zachry
491. Zacory
492. Zaevian
493. Zaimar
494. Zaiyden
495. Zaveion
496. Zerick
497. Ziion
498. Zirui
499. Ziyang
500. Zyrin

Over 400 Unique Girls' Names

A

1. Aamyah
2. Aarion
3. Abbagale
4. Abhigna
5. Abisha
6. Abryanna
7. Adallyn
8. Adar
9. Adelade
10. Adhithi
11. Adithri
12. Adreonna
13. Adynn
14. Aevah
15. Agness
16. Ahmara
17. Aimen
18. Aireona
19. Aiylah
20. Alaniz
21. Aleezah
22. Aleira
23. Alesi
24. Alieah
25. Alienna
26. Alik
27. Allaynah
28. Allisa
29. Allivia
30. Amai
31. Amaka
32. Amaleah
33. Amane
34. Ambrie
35. Ameeyah
36. Amilea
37. Anabelen
38. Anadia
39. Anaiis
40. Anaveah
41. Andressa
42. Angee
43. Angeni
44. Anndee
45. Annelyn
46. Antoria
47. Anuoluwa
48. Anyssia
49. Apurva
50. Aracelli
51. Aramis
52. Arieon
53. Armiyah
54. Arra
55. Aryauna
56. Aryian
57. Astryd
58. Asuna
59. Athenamarie

60. Aubreonna
61. Aubrieanna
62. Aubriona
63. Avaclaire
64. Avaiya
65. Avelin
66. Avynn
67. Ayin
68. Aylissa
69. Ayrian
70. Ayten
71. Ayvree
72. Ayvrie
73. Azora
74. Azyla

B

75. Baela
76. Baisley
77. Baja
78. Bambi
79. Bellina
80. Bethaney
81. Betzayda
82. Beverley
83. Biana
84. Bitia
85. Bradlie
86. Brandalynn
87. Breigh
88. Brielee
89. Britian
90. Britlyn
91. Briyonna
92. Brookleigh
93. Brookley
94. Byrdie

C

95. Cailie
96. Camiah
97. Cariel
98. Carlaya
99. Carliyah
100. Casiyah
101. Cataliya
102. Cayle
103. Ceci
104. Chamille
105. Charizma
106. Chastin
107. Claramae
108. Cristaly

D

109. Daegan
110. Daleysi
111. Dameria
112. Damiracle
113. Daniely
114. Darshi
115. Dashawna
116. Dazie
117. Denisa

118. Diamonique
119. Dianelys
120. Dimitra
121. Dollie
122. Donovan
123. Dreana
124. Dublin

E

125. Eilonwy
126. Eirian
127. Elanny
128. Elhana
129. Elias
130. Elliekate
131. Ellisa
132. Elysian
133. Emanni
134. Emelee
135. Emyri
136. Epic
137. Esmerie
138. Estel
139. Esveidy
140. Ettie
141. Eversyn
142. Ewaoluwa

F

143. Faige
144. Fallan
145. Farrell
146. Felix
147. Fiorenza
148. Franyelis
149. Fynn

G

150. Gabreilla
151. Gavyn
152. Geetika
153. Giannarose
154. Giannina
155. Giulliana
156. Guneet
157. Gurseerat
158. Gwenyvere

H

159. Hadara
160. Hade
161. Hadya
162. Halsey
163. Hanako
164. Harneet
165. Harseerat
166. Havanah
167. Hawraa
168. Hayoon
169. Hazen
170. Hela
171. Heleyna

172. Helia
173. Helin
174. Hidayah
175. Hind
176. Hiromi
177. Hridya
178. Humayra

I

179. Icesis
180. Illana
181. Iqlas
182. Isel
183. Isobelle
184. Ivary

J

185. Jaasia
186. Jacoba
187. Jadayah
188. Jaecia
189. Jaelyne
190. Jahzarra
191. Jakai
192. Jakalyn
193. Jakaria
194. Jakaya
195. Jalaila
196. Jalayshia
197. Jalene
198. Janye
199. Jasira
200. Jawaher
201. Jayceonna
202. Jaylianiz
203. Jayonni
204. Jazaiya
205. Jazirah
206. Jeanetta
207. Jeniveve
208. Jenson
209. Jerra
210. Jessel
211. Jestina
212. Jhaniya
213. Jillianne
214. Jisella
215. Jisha
216. Jocilynn
217. Joselle
218. Joshalynn
219. Josselynn
220. Jozalynn
221. Jraya
222. Judie
223. Juel
224. Juliannie
225. Jura
226. Justyne
227. Jwan

K

228. Kacia
229. Kadijah

230. Kaegan
231. Kairy
232. Kaithlynn
233. Kaizleigh
234. Kalaiah
235. Kalonie
236. Kambrya
237. Kamijah
238. Kamlyn
239. Kannon
240. Karelyn
241. Karidee
242. Kariya
243. Kashish
244. Katrine
245. Kaycen
246. Kayelle
247. Kayin
248. Kayleeh
249. Kaziya
250. Kealohilani
251. Keaysia
252. Keelia
253. Kemariah
254. Kemyra
255. Kennison
256. Kenz
257. Kesia
258. Keyarah
259. Keymiah
260. Khady
261. Khaleya
262. Khyara
263. Kimmi
264. Kimori
265. Kiyani
266. Kiylah
267. Kla
268. Kolbe
269. Konner
270. Kortana
271. Krithika
272. Kumari
273. Ky
274. Kylise
275. Kyoko

L

276. Labiba
277. Laelyn
278. Laighla
279. Lakelee
280. Lanaea
281. Lanier
282. Lanye
283. Lanylah
284. Lauralyn
285. Layten
286. Leea
287. Leelani
288. Leeona
289. Leesa
290. Lenamarie
291. Lenya
292. Leonardo
293. Liley
294. Lilyani
295. Lilyannah

296. Lilymarie
297. Lindee
298. Lindsi
299. Lizandra
300. Lizbet
301. Lizett
302. Louiza
303. Lucian
304. Lulabelle
305. Lyndley
306. Lynett

M

307. Macilyn
308. Madee
309. Madisan
310. Maebrie
311. Maiara
312. Maisa
313. Makhya
314. Maki
315. Maleaha
316. Manika
317. Manisha
318. Marea
319. Margareth
320. Marieme
321. Marisha
322. Mariyana
323. Marybel
324. Maryse
325. Matteo
326. Mavie
327. Mckinze
328. Mckinzey
329. Meiqi
330. Melita
331. Melvina
332. Micahya
333. Mickinley
334. Mieko
335. Mikal
336. Miku
337. Mileyshka
338. Millian
339. Miraj
340. Mirajane
341. Morah
342. Morley

N

343. Nadina
344. Nanaakua
345. Nashay
346. Natascha
347. Nayali
348. Necha
349. Neftali
350. Nelliel
351. Nenah
352. Neveya
353. Neymar
354. Neysha
355. Ni
356. Nicci
357. Nigella

358. Nikiah
359. Nikyla
360. Nisreen
361. Nneka
362. Noran
363. Nouran
364. Nuriyah
365. Nyemiah
366. Nyriah

O

367. Oluwatise
368. Otylia
369. Ourania
370. Owynn
371. Oyindamola
372. Ozara

P

373. Paitin
374. Penelopea
375. Persephany
376. Petrona
377. Petunia
378. Pretty

Q

379. Quentin
380. Quetzally

R

381. Raeden
382. Raegin
383. Raika
384. Raye
385. Rayli
386. Rayssa
387. Rei
388. Reyanna
389. Riko
390. Rily
391. Riyaq
392. Roniah
393. Rosalei
394. Rosilyn
395. Rosilynn
396. Rossie
397. Rozalin
398. Rozie
399. Ruman
400. Rumer

S

401. Saanjh
402. Saanvika
403. Sadan
404. Saedi
405. Safiye
406. Sahej
407. Sahvanna
408. Saleema

409. Samay
410. Sanaiyah
411. Sanjuana
412. Sarem
413. Savya
414. Sayumi
415. Seela
416. Sehar
417. Semia
418. Serine
419. Shadin
420. Shaeley
421. Shahed
422. Shaley
423. Shannia
424. Shaylea
425. Shir
426. Sionna
427. Skyana
428. Smrithi
429. Solea
430. Somtochukwu
431. Sorelle
432. Southern
433. Stonie
434. Suhavi
435. Sukhman
436. Suniya
437. Surayah
438. Swathi
439. Szofia

T

440. Tabbitha
441. Taedyn
442. Tahel
443. Taijah
444. Tailah
445. Taiwo
446. Taizley
447. Takylah
448. Taly
449. Tamlyn
450. Taneah
451. Tashawna
452. Tayelor
453. Tayli
454. Teniyah
455. Tennasyn
456. Torian
457. Trace
458. Trysten
459. Tylan
460. Tylor
461. Tynia
462. Tynlie

U

463. Urijah

V

464. Vainavi
465. Vaishvi
466. Valetina

467. Varna
468. Vedhika
469. Versavia
470. Veyah
471. Violetrose

W

---

472. Whitaker

X

---

473. Xareny
474. Xaylie
475. Xiclali
476. Xitllali

Y

---

477. Yahna
478. Yalexi
479. Yariza
480. Yazayra
481. Yiru
482. Yoko
483. Yu
484. Yuktha
485. Yvonna

Z

---

486. Zaelah
487. Zahriah
488. Zaiden
489. Zamoni
490. Zandrea
491. Zanovia
492. Zarae
493. Zarahy
494. Zayanah
495. Zaydah
496. Zeila
497. Zellah
498. Zoeymarie
499. Zoree
500. Zyriyah

Chapter 12: Over 400 Gender-Neutral Names

Are you keeping your baby's gender a secret from yourself? Do you disagree with classic gender norms?

When choosing a name for your child, you may want to consider a name that doesn't specify a gender.

While names tend to lean towards one gender or the other, these names are commonly used for children of either gender.

A

1. Aaron
2. Addison
3. Ade
4. Ainsley
5. Akachi
6. Akira
7. Aldus
8. Alex
9. Alexis
10. Almas
11. Amal
12. Amari
13. Amets
14. An
15. Anantha
16. Andie
17. Andy
18. Angel
19. Aran
20. Arden
21. Ariel
22. Arlie
23. Ash
24. Ashley
25. Ashton
26. Aston
27. Aubrey
28. Avery
29. Ayo
30. Azar
31. Azariah

B

32. Bailey
33. Bernie
34. Bertie
35. Billie

36. Blair
37. Blake
38. Blythe
39. Bobbie
40. Brady
41. Brett
42. Brook

C

43. Cam
44. Cameron
45. Camille
46. Cande
47. Carey
48. Carol
49. Caron
50. Carson
51. Carter
52. Cary
53. Casey
54. Cassidy
55. Celestine
56. Chandra
57. Chang
58. Channing
59. Charley
60. Charlie
61. Chen
62. Cheng
63. Cheyenne
64. Chin
65. Chinwe
66. Chris
67. Coby
68. Connie
69. Corin
70. Cruz

D

71. Dakota
72. Dallas
73. Dale
74. Dana
75. Darby
76. Darcy
77. Darian
78. Dell
79. Devon
80. Dian
81. Dominique
82. Drew
83. Dylan

E

84. Eddie
85. Eden
86. Erian
87. Eka
88. Eko
89. Elliott
90. Emerson
91. Emery
92. Emory
93. Ennis

F

94. Farah
95. Fergie
96. Finley
97. Flann
98. Flannery
99. Florence
100. Fran
101. Francis
102. Frankie
103. Franny
104. Freddie
105. Fu

G

106. Gabby
107. Garnet
108. Gayle
109. Georgie
110. Gerry
111. Greer
112. Gulshan
113. Guo

H

114. Hadar
115. Hadley
116. Hai
117. Hanne
118. Haris
119. Harley
120. Harlow
121. Harper
122. Haru
123. Haven
124. Hayden
125. Heike
126. Hennie
127. Hikaru
128. Huan
129. Hui
130. Hunter

I

131. Ihab
132. Ihsan
133. Imani
134. Indiana
135. Indigo
136. Innes
137. Ismat
138. Issy

J

139. Jackie
140. Jaden
141. Jadyn
142. Jaffe
143. Jamie

144. Jaya
145. Jaylen
146. Jayne
147. Jeong
148. Jerry
149. Jess
150. Jian
151. Jin
152. Jo
153. Jody
154. Joey
155. Jojo
156. Jools
157. Jordan
158. Jordyn
159. Joss
160. Joyce
161. Jules
162. Jun
163. Justice
164. Justy
165. Jyoti

K

166. Kaede
167. Kagiso
168. Kai
169. Kaipo
170. Kamala
171. Kamon
172. Kamryn
173. Kaoru
174. Karam
175. Karter
176. Kasey
177. Kayden
178. Keahi
179. Kealoha
180. Keanu
181. Keelan
182. Kelcey
183. Kelly
184. Kelsey
185. Kendal
186. Kennedy
187. Kenzie
188. Kerry
189. Keshet
190. Ki
191. Kim
192. Kiran
193. Konani
194. Kris
195. Kun
196. Kyo
197. Kyung

L

198. Landry
199. Lauren
200. Laverne
201. Lee
202. Lehua
203. Leigh
204. Leighton
205. Lennon

206. Lesley
207. Leslie
208. Li
209. Lin
210. Lindsay
211. Lindsey
212. Lindy
213. Ling
214. Logan
215. London
216. Lor
217. Loren
218. Loreto
219. Lou
220. Lux
221. Lynn
222. Lyric

M

---

223. Mackenzie
224. Madison
225. Mahlah
226. Makana
227. Makara
228. Makena
229. Makoto
230. Malak
231. Manais
232. Manu
233. Maram
234. Marley
235. Martie
236. Mattie
237. Maui
238. Meade
239. Mel
240. Meredith
241. Merle
242. Micah
243. Micaiah
244. Michi
245. Mickey
246. Mies
247. Milan
248. Min
249. Ming
250. Modeste
251. Mohana
252. Monet
253. Montana
254. Mor
255. Moran
256. Morgan
257. Mu
258. Murphy

N

---

259. Meong
260. Nalani
261. Naomi
262. Narcisse
263. Naseem
264. Nasim
265. Nat

266. Neelam
267. Neo
268. Nicky
269. Nika
270. Nikora
271. Nilam
272. Nima
273. Nimat
274. Ning
275. Nithya
276. Noam
277. Noga
278. Nogah
279. Noy
280. Nuka
281. Nur

O

---

282. Oakley
283. Odalis
284. Odell
285. Ofir
286. Ofra
287. Ollie
288. Oluchi
289. Omega
290. Omid
291. Or
292. Ora
293. Ori

P

---

294. Padma
295. Parker
296. Parris
297. Pat
298. Patsy
299. Payton
300. Paz
301. Petia
302. Petya
303. Peyton
304. Phoenix
305. Pich
306. Ping
307. Placide
308. Presley
309. Prudence
310. Puck
311. Purdie

Q

---

312. Qing
313. Quinn

R

---

314. Rahat
315. Rain
316. Raine

317. Randy
318. Raven
319. Ravid
320. Rayan
321. Raz
322. Reagan
323. Reese
324. Reilly
325. Remington
326. Remy
327. Ren
328. Rene
329. Reyes
330. Ricki
331. Riley
332. Rini
333. River
334. Robbie
335. Robin
336. Ron
337. Rong
338. Rory
339. Rosario
340. Roshan
341. Rotem
342. Rowan
343. Ru
344. Rudo
345. Rutendo
346. Ryan
347. Rylan
348. Rylee

S

349. Sage
350. Sal
351. Sam
352. Sammie
353. Sammy
354. Sandy
355. Sang
356. Sascha
357. Sashi
358. Satchel
359. Sawyer
360. Selby
361. Seong
362. September
363. Sequoia
364. Seung
365. Sevan
366. Shalev
367. Shani
368. Shannon
369. Shashi
370. Shay
371. Shea
372. Shelby
373. Shelley
374. Shelly
375. Sheridan
376. Shi
377. Shiloh
378. Shinobu
379. Shun
380. Shura

381. Sidney
382. Sigi
383. Skylar
384. Skyler
385. Slava
386. Sophea
387. Sora
388. Sparrow
389. Stacey
390. Stacy
391. Stav
392. Steph
393. Stevie
394. Storm
395. Su
396. Sunan
397. Sung
398. Sydney

T

---

399. Taegan
400. Tai
401. Tal
402. Tam
403. Tatum
404. Tayler
405. Taylor
406. Teagan
407. Temple
408. Terry
409. Themba
410. Tibby
411. Tivoli
412. Toby
413. Tommie
414. Tracey
415. Tracy
416. Tri

U

---

417. Ulli

V

---

418. Val
419. Vanja
420. Vanna
421. Vasilica
422. Vic
423. Vieno
424. Vinh

W

---

425. Wei
426. Whitney
427. Wil
428. Willie
429. Willy
430. Wu
431. Wynne

X

432. Xiang
433. Xun

Y

434. Yafe
435. Yaffe
436. Yanick
437. Yannic
438. Yannick
439. Yarden
440. Yasu
441. Yeong
442. Yi
443. Yong
444. Yoon
445. Yoshi
446. Young
447. Yuki
448. Yun
449. Yuu

Z

450. Zan
451. Zheng
452. Zhenya
453. Zhi
454. Zhong
455. Zhou
456. Zion

Made in the USA
Middletown, DE
17 March 2016